THAI DREAMINGS

Australian Aboriginal Inspirations in the Paintings of Kitti Narod

Felicity A. Rodner

Thai Dreamings. Australian Aboriginal Inspirations in the Paintings of Kitti Narod was published by Felicity A. Rodner under the auspices of Thai Fine Art Ltd and printed by Permanent Printing Ltd in Hong Kong. 2005.

ISBN: 0-9551442-0-5
        978-0-9551442-0-2

*I am simply a painter, who shares
this world of ours, as a small unit
in human society, paying my due
and hoping to contribute by a small
measure to the planet earth.*
Chalermchai Kositpipat

*Thai artists seem to have a gift for
synthesizing several styles into their
own quintessential creations.*
Apinan Poshyananda

THAI DREAMINGS
Australian Aboriginal Inspirations in the Paintings of Kitti Narod

From A to B -- Australia to Bangkok

It seems a far cry from the hustle and bustle of Bangkok's city streets to Aboriginal Australia's endless horizons, but dreaming knows no boundaries in time and space, and a young Thai painter, Kitti Narod, has captured motifs and techniques from native Australian art and transposed these uniquely into his own Thai imagery using acrylic paint on canvas. The result is a vibrant palette where forms and textures coalesce in images drawn from nature and are transformed by Kitti's artistic imagination to express his "dreaming", his own personal vision of his world, his life and the world he shares with us, his viewers.

A young Bangkok painter making use of native pictorial techniques from a country he has never even visited certainly seems to be an unusual proposition, but we have to remember that Thai painters have long been in the habit of adopting themes and styles from foreign traditions and successfully developing these into a tradition of their own. Following a flurry of prehistoric artistic activity in Thailand, the first major foreign influence in Thai art was that of India. Between the first and sixth centuries AD, Thai art is characterised by the importation or imitation of Indian sculptures and styles which initially served the Hindu religion followed by most people at that time and which were to retain their influence for the following thousand years or so. As Buddhism gradually displaced Hinduism in Thailand, the Indian techniques and motifs adopted by Thai builders and artists were seamlessly adapted to create temples and images dedicated to the Lord Buddha.

Art at this time was dominated by royal patronage and its inspiration was Theravada Buddhism, a condition that persisted well into the twentieth century. The temple complex was the focal point of all communities, and the act of funding or decorating a temple structure ensured merit for the patron or maker that would carry him through to a better life in his next reincarnation. Buddhism remains, even in our materialistic age, an integral part of Thai life, and it is to this day an honour and challenge for a painter to collaborate in the design or decoration of a Buddhist temple. One of

Thailand's most eminent painters, Chalermchai Kositpipat, "Arjarn" or "Master" of his art, has made a major contribution to the murals of the Thai Buddhist temple, Wat Buddhapadipa, in Wimbledon, London, and is currently fully committed to the design, construction and decoration of his own Wat Rong Khun in northern Thailand. Though this temple complex in white and silver is very much Chalermchai's own personal style, the artist pays homage to tradition in that he intends to dedicate his completed creation to His Majesty the King of Thailand.

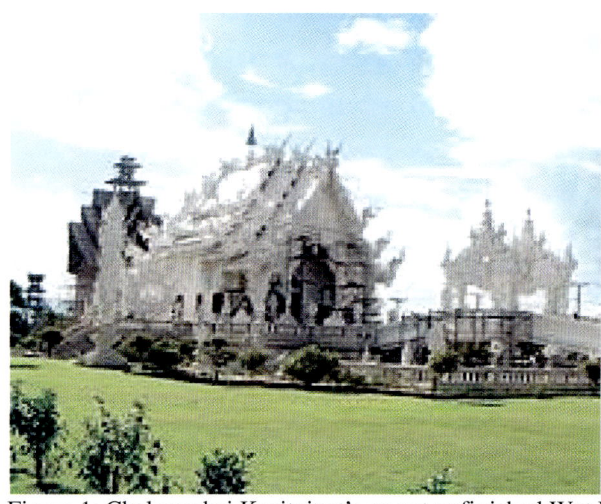
Figure 1: Chalermchai Kositpipat's as yet unfinished Wat Rong Khun
in northern Thailand. www.bangkokpost.co.th for 28-7-2005.

Temple murals, initially Indian in inspiration, were the first painted works in the history of Thai art. Although narrow in range and subject-matter and flatly devoid of perspective or shading, these murals were vital, vivid and aesthetically pleasing as well as religiously correct. Unfortunately, few survive: fire, smoke, rain from above and rising damp from below have all but annihilated the fragile tempera paintings. As Indian influence waned, Mon, or Dvaravati, indigenous art from the Central Plains area expanded through Thailand, leaving us a wealth of seated Buddha images and the characteristic Dhammachakra, or Wheel of Buddhist Law sculptures. Following the Dvaravati school, the Srivijava sophisticated stone and bronze sculptures come to us from the Hinduised invaders from Central Java, but little else survives in Thailand of these thirteenth-century visitors.

Thailand, unlike many of her immediate neighbours such as Vietnam, Cambodia, Malaysia or Myanmar (Burma), has never been colonised or occupied by a foreign power. Migration, trade and war, however, have encouraged a continuous bombardment of foreign influences which have been assimilated over time into the Thai culture to a greater or lesser extent.

Thailand has never been inclined to close her borders; the country is in fact very receptive to thoughts, trends and styles from abroad, and indeed welcomes foreign philosophies and religions with true Buddhist equanimity. Cambodian (Khmer) influences were felt in the central and north-eastern areas of Thailand through the seventh to fourteenth centuries. For the first three hundred years or so of this period, Khmer temples or monuments were erected by Cambodian artists and by Thais following the Cambodian style, which was then gradually assimilated into the Thai tradition as the Lop Buri school of architecture and sculpture. No painting from this period survives, although the Khmer influence as such was strong in the Lanna kingdom of northern Thailand, and the almond-shaped eyes and full-lipped Khmer smile are unforgotten stylistic elements in Thai painting even now. Borirak Giettgamjorn's **Khmer Bas Relief** testifies to a continuing Khmer tradition in contemporary Thai painting.

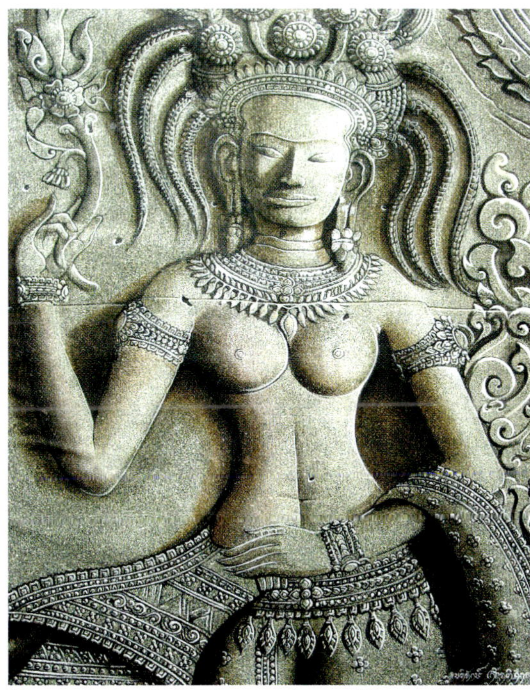

Figure 2: Borirak Giettgamjorn: *Khmer Bas Relief* (2004). 60 x 60 cm. Acrylic on canvas.

Thematic and stylistic influences from India and Cambodia gradually synthesized into Thai artistry to produce the sophisticated architecture, statuary and ceramics of the mature Sukhothai period. Of the temple murals, unfortunately, the few scraps of paint still adhering to the niche walls of the Wat Chedi Jet Thaew in Si Satchanalai are all that survive from the Sukhothai school. Subsequent Ayutthayan murals depicting the life of Buddha, Ramakien scenes and similar classical themes fared better. The

Phetchaburi murals dating from the mid-eighteenth century interestingly include contemporary visitors to Thailand among the figures depicted: bearded and costumed Arab and European figures contrast with local elephants and Thai worshipers before the figure of the Lord Buddha who stands framed by the flames of his enlightenment.

Chinese art has similarly penetrated Thai art and culture through the ages via pilgrimages, migrations, political, commercial and cultural contacts. By the mid-nineteenth century, considerable immigration to Thailand from China had exerted such artistic influence that Chinese art had come to be associated with the extremely prestigious "Preferred Royal Style". Strong links bind Thai and Chinese painting to this day. Soraya Runckel was born in Bangkok, studied Chinese brush painting, lived for three years in Beijing and now paints and sells her work in the USA; she is but one of many Thai painters whose work is happily indebted to Chinese influences.

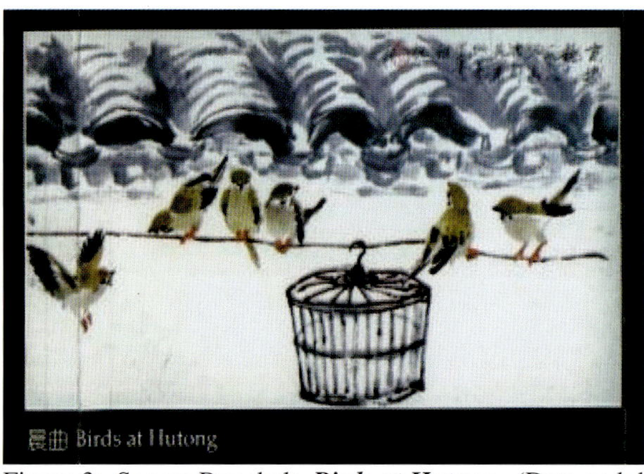

Figure 3: Soraya Runckel: ***Birds at Hutong***. (Date and dimensions unknown). Chinese Brush Painting on paper. www.asia-art.net

Once foreign styles have been woven into the fabric of Thai art, they become established and conventional and so, in an ever-changing world, a window is then opened for new, less conventional foreign influences to enter the scene. Thus, mid-nineteenth century Bangkok, by now Siam's capital following the fall from prominence of Sukhothai and then Ayutthaya, was ripe for stylistic innovation, and this innovation came not from India, China or any other Asian source. It came from Western Europe. Political and commercial relations with Europe familiarised Thai high society with western styles and architecture. Setting up Bangkok as the new capital involved building splendid royal palaces and Buddhist temples representative of the wealth and importance of the ruling Chakri dynasty. Western architectural elements, such as Doric and Ionic columns, domes and

4

decorative chandeliers, were royally preferred and highly visible. This was no purist imitation, however: western arched windows and classical European columns supporting three-headed mythological Thai elephants rubbed shoulders with traditional Siamese gilded spires; European chandeliers jostled nine-tiered royal umbrellas in a hybrid display unfettered by budget considerations or an organic understanding of what western styles really meant. Out of chaos order emerged, however, and with time the initially over-emphatic westernisation of Thai style resolved itself into a fruitful cross-cultural creativity that continues to evolve to the present day.

The man credited with being the father of modern art in Thailand was an Italian sculptor by the name of Corrado Feroci, who, invited to Bangkok in 1924 by King Rama VI (1910-1925) to teach Thai artisans how to cast bronze monuments of their Kings and heroes (a cheaper and more creative alternative to importing huge, ready-made statues all the way from Europe), ended up staying until his death in 1962, taking the Thai name, Silpa Bhirasri, and founding the nation's first fine arts school, later to become Bangkok's Silpakorn University. Feroci exerted an incalculable influence on the formation of young Thai artists in the twentieth century. His aim was to educate a new generation of sculptors and painters in the theory and practice of western modern art without at the same time abandoning the close traditional bond between fine art and handicraft that had always existed in Thailand. His influence encouraged experimentation in Impressionism, Realism, Cubism, Expressionism, Abstract Impressionism, landscape painting and even portraiture, which was an art-form quite alien to Thai tradition. This artistic surge into modernity was mirrored in Thailand's political and social condition. A 1932 coup d'état forced the abolition of the hitherto absolute monarchy in favour of a constitutional monarchy with all the trappings of western democracy. Western fads, fashions, taste and trinkets were now all the rage.

But all good things must come to an end, as do all bad ones, for that matter, and Thai voices began to be raised against the westernisation of their art and culture. Some resented modernity's drastic innovations; many feared for the future of traditional Thai subjects and styles in art; others regarded adoption of western styles as mere empty imitation, devoid of artistic meaning or individuality. This kind of reaction, which came to a head in the 1960s and was then exacerbated by the effect and implications of the Vietnam War, clashed with those who still pushed wholeheartedly for western-style modernity. Art and society destabilised. A political-social uprising in 1973 was punished by suppressive government measures in 1976. Artists in revolt meanwhile continued to make their voices heard:

some entrenched themselves in the older, traditional themes and styles; others painted condemnations of the Americanisation of the East and the destructive folly of war. Feroci and modernisation had left their indelible mark, however. These artistic condemnations of western influences were painted in western terms, using western conventions. Thus, Thamask Booncherd, for example, rails against the west in Futurist, cartoon-like images, his stripe-vested American eagle brandishing a machine-gun and a bag of dollar bills while raining bullets and bombs down on the Thai flag laid out below it.

As the Vietnam War came to an end and peace and prosperity returned to south-east Asia, modern art in Thailand began to become institutionalised. The Fine Arts University had already been established in 1943; the League of Artists and the Society of Painters and Sculptors were founded and had flourished for over a decade. Exhibitions, competitions and prizes encouraged young artists. Silpakorn University opened its own art gallery in 1979, whilst Chulalongkorn University, also in Bangkok, set up its Faculty of Fine and Applied Arts in 1983. Chiang Mai University opened its own Fine Arts Faculty in the same year, and this northern city since 1998 hosts the Chiang Mai University Art Museum. The Bhirasri Institute of Modern Art encouraged modern artists in Bangkok until it closed for lack of funds.

Funding for art is in fact a critical issue in Thailand. In the economic boom of the 1980s, government and corporate sponsorship fostered artistic production of every kind, the downside of this situation being, of course, that artists were to some extent conditioned by their patrons, rather as the royal and religious patrons of earlier centuries had determined the style and content of the works they had commissioned. The 1997 economic crisis and collapse in Asia effectively eliminated government and corporate funding for art in Thailand. The ensuing bankruptcies, unemployment, economic depression and uncertainty predictably depressed private collectors, galleries and other exhibition spaces as well. Powerful priorities do not even now favour modern art. A Bangkok Metropolitan Arts Centre built in the 1990s ended up as 80% shopping mall, with only the small remaining portion devoted to artworks. Government did establish an Office of Contemporary Art and Culture in 2003, but the fact remains that, to this day, luxury hotels, the more prosperous shopping centres, small private galleries and markets are where modern Thai art is most visibly shown on a commercial scale.

Despite the rise and fall of art on the commercial market, however, painters and sculptors continue to create, and modern forms of artistic expression have taken firm root in Thailand. When these are combined and contrasted with the strictly traditional styles and motifs that are still very much alive, together with what we might call a surrealist-traditional dedication to Buddhist themes, we understand why the contemporary art scene in Thailand offers a veritable cornucopia of artworks to suit every possible taste and inclination.

There are, for example, expressions of political and social protest. The satin-suited "Pink Man" who pushes his shopping trolley across Manit Sriwanichpoom's canvases humorously parodies western materialism. Where Manit laments his own feelings of alienation in a materialistic world, Manop Suwanpinta rages against institutionalised egotism as it threatens our planet's natural resources. Vichoke Mukdamanee similarly dedicates his mixed media hangings and installations to a protest against ecological devastation, particularly in the forests of northern Thailand. "Happenings" and installations are particularly appropriate for social protest. Chumpon Apisuk's 1987-1988 "happening/pure communication" staged at various venues involved the artist-shaman standing amidst chairs, bricks and assembled junk, mumbling deliriously, drinking pig's blood and smashing assorted objects in a protest against materialism's attack on Thailand's major cities.

There are experiments with easily identifiable western subjects and styles. Fua Haribhitak, painting in the mid-1950s, tried his hand more or less successfully with Impressionism in his seascape, *Fraglioni Rocks, Capri*, and with Cubism in his *Chromatic Variations* and *Blue-Green*. Abstract compositions abound. Chavalit Soemprungsuk's *Untitled* (1990) convincingly superimposes textured colour-blocks in red, white and blue. Wallaya Rattanapirom's *Season* triptych combines a feminine, pastel palette with lightly sketched floral forms to convey her homeland's three-season

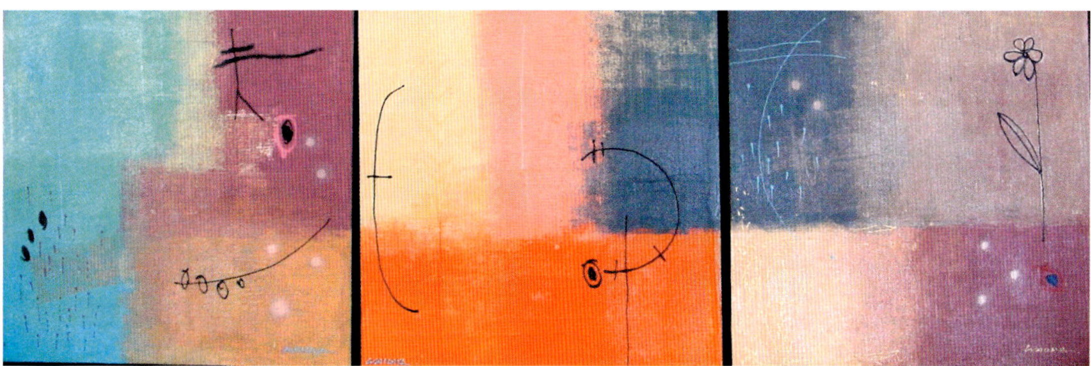

Figure 4: Wallaya Rattanapirom: *Season* (2005). Each canvas 38 x 38 cm. Acrylic on canvas. (Private collection).

climate, which is not, as you might imagine, "hot", "hotter" and "hottest", but rather "rainy", "hot" and (in tropical terms) "cool". The eminent Thai art critic, Apinan Poshyananda, detects a strong affinity between Buddhism and Abstract art. The Buddhist's seeking to transcend the material in his approach to spiritual truth revels in reducing plastic structures to the fundamental elements of visual perception, overcoming chaos through simplicity and clarity.

Thai painting, both ancient and modern, uniquely combines vivid colours with textures, gold leaf and an intricacy of pattern and design that can baffle and fascinate the western viewer. There are, however, modern experiments with more subdued, typically northern-European effects and themes. Nikorn U-aksorn took early retirement from his Thai Oil Refinery position to devote himself professionally to watercolour painting. He has successfully exhibited and sold abroad and is President of the Thai Watercolour Association. Nikon's subjects and artistic vision are strikingly non-Thai.

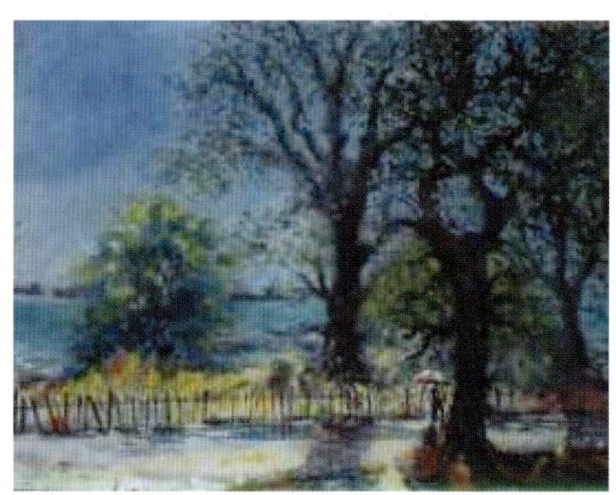

Figure 5: Nikorn U-aksorn: *A Walk in the Rain*. Date unknown. 16 x 22 inches. Watercolour on paper. www.asia-art.net.

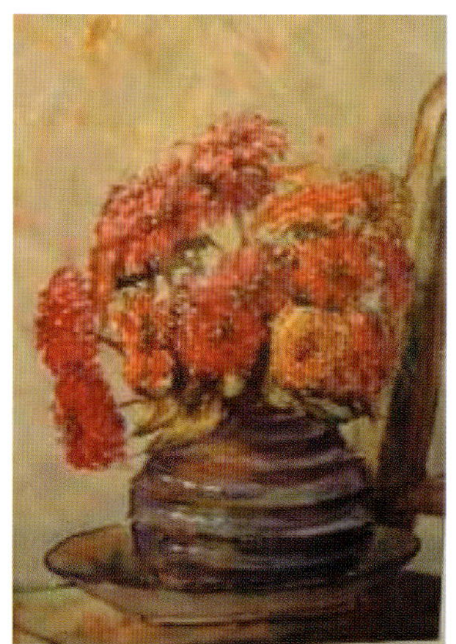

Figure 6: Nikorn U-aksorn: *Flowers*. Date unknown. 16 x 22 inches. Watercolour on paper. www.asia-art.net

Pornchai Lerttamasiri has intriguingly rendered native Thai landscapes, riverscapes and city views, which are not characteristic motifs in Thai paintings, using an experimental medium that is uniquely his own. Pornchai originally painted in watercolour on paper. Seeking a subdued, sepia effect, he tried staining his paper with tea or coffee and then attempted painting entirely with tea instead of paint. Tea proving to be too wishy-washy, however, Pornchai then tried a solution of sodium permanganate. He was pleased with the purplish-brown, antique-style effects this produced until purchasers of his paintings brought them back to him after a few months complaining that the whole picture had faded off the paper. Experiments painting with a solution of coffee and water proved less embarrassing. Getting the proportions right was not easy (using too much coffee causes the image to peel off the paper or go mouldy with time), but Pornchai is now confident that his new technique renders his scenes in attractively suitable soft, muted tones that will stand the test of time and give his audience something new and creative, close to their daily lives and at the same time artistically distanced from reality.

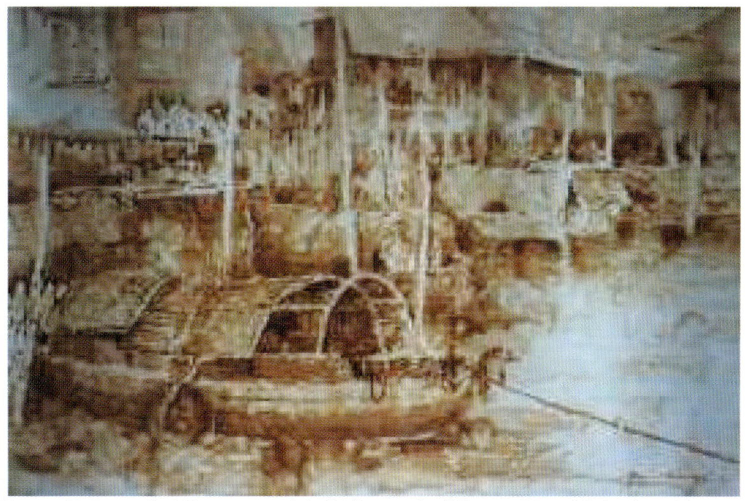

Figure 7: Pornchai Lerttamasiri: *Life on the Water*. 20 x 30 inches (date unknown). Coffee and water solution on watercolour paper. www.asia-art.net.

Women are strong on the Thai art front. Pinaree Sanpitak expressly aims to give the viewer a glimpse into woman's inner being. Her mixed media ***Golden Womb*** (1997) pales by comparison with her 200-unit installation of giant, synthetic-fibre breasts (***Noon-nom***, 2001-2002). Pinaree's anatomical insinuations are pleasant to behold by comparison with Araya Rasdjarmrearnsook's shockingly depressing installations. Her ***The Dinner with Cancer*** (1993), a mixed-media installation featuring a stripped hospital bed standing on a dirty, damp floor surrounded by what looks like the debris of sickness and death, is evocative in the extreme, but an artwork that probably most viewers would not want to look at more than once. Winya Jantaporn, by contrast, renders traditional themes with a passionate dexterity and gift for colour and detail that single her out as one of the most proficient young women painting in Bangkok today.

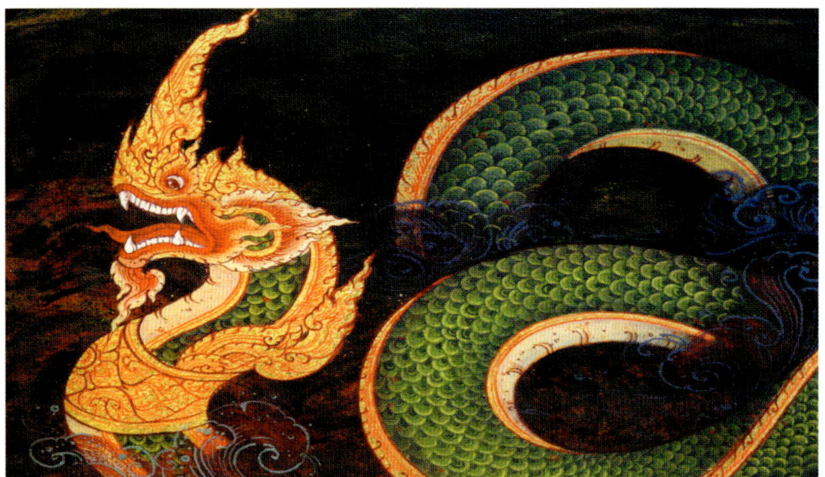

Figure 8: Winya Jantaporn: *Naga* (2005). 20 x 40 cm. Acrylic on canvas. (Detail). (Private collection)

Chalermchai Kositpipat, in addition to his contemporary contribution to temple construction and decoration within and outside of Thailand, is undoubtedly one of today's most prestigious painters of traditional Thai and Buddhist themes. His idiosyncratically modern visions glow with a surreal dynamic born of religious faith and devotion, whilst his painstakingly minute detail draws the viewer ever closer to the work and into the painter's personal revelation.

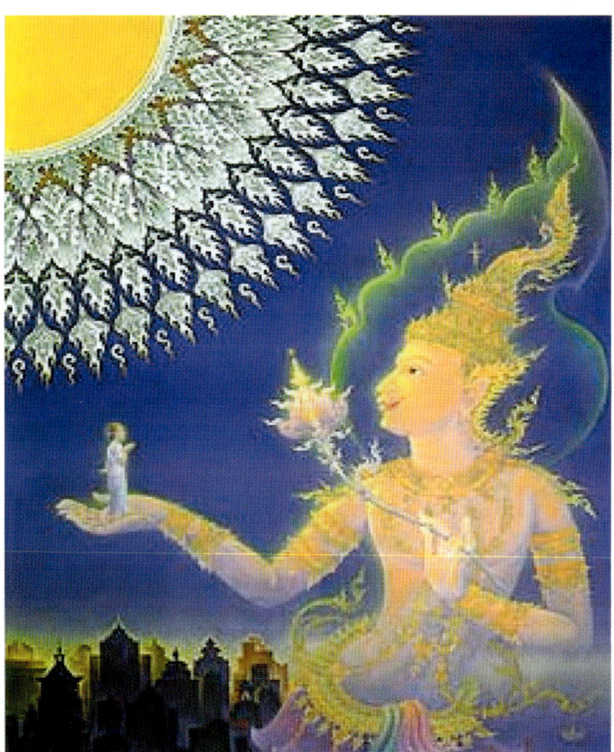

Figure 9: Chalermchai Kositpipat: *Mind to Mind* (1994). 120 x 90 cm. Acrylic and pencil on canvas. www.rama9art.org.

10

Kitti Narod admits to enjoying and being influenced by traditional, Indian-style murals and by Byzantine mosaics, but his dot-on-dot acrylics on canvas do not draw directly on Indian, Chinese, western or even traditional Thai models. Thai painting's open and accepting attitude to foreign influences is mirrored differently in Kitti's work. He draws inspiration from the art of Aboriginal Australia. The 1980s and 1990s cemented relations between Thailand and Australia specifically within the Asia-Pacific region via a series of exhibitions of Australian contemporary and Aboriginal art in Bangkok, whilst Thai artists have reciprocated at Australian venues and Australian artists have worked with students at the Chiang Mai and Silpakorn Universities. Kitti's first encounters with Australian indigenous art via the Discovery Channel on television, together with some experimentation with aboriginal dot techniques while at art school, led him to perfect the method in 2001 for his own artistic purposes.

Australian Aboriginal rock paintings date from between forty and fifty thousand years ago, when the Aboriginal people are thought to have first arrived in Australia from south-east Asia. These rock paintings, some geometric, combining circular and linear motifs, others depicting wallabies, kangaroos or human figures, are an important source of information on prehistoric Australia. They are thus anthropologically informative, but they are also art and mystery. When taken together with designs drawn or painted on the land, on bark, wood or human bodies or hewn into cave walls, the rock paintings to this day convey the Aboriginal spiritual, natural and moral order of time and the cosmos, together with a supra-natural mapping through time and space of their land, their history, their system of kinship, their past, present and future.

Aboriginal "Dreamings" encompass time from before the earth's creation to beyond human memory or imagination. The word "Dreamings" thus means in the context of Aboriginal art much more than the simple English word conveys to us at first hearing. The Dreaming depicts the epic achievements of the supernatural creator-ancestors, both human and non-human in form, that laid down the shapes of the Aboriginal lands and determined the ideological framework within which groups and individuals are to behave socially and religiously. As befits a Dreaming, the Aboriginal drawings and designs are intentionally ambiguous, relying on inconclusive iconographies and layers of multiple meaning that depend for their interpretation on the insider knowledge of both artist and observer. Ritual and ancestral landscapes are not open books for all and sundry to read. The deepest levels of meaning are reserved only for the select initiates; more mundane levels of significance are revealed to the casual viewer. This includes the topographical content of the Dreamings, which map out for those in the know the ancestral paths travelled by supernatural creators and which determine at the same time the social and kinship order of the very diverse social groupings scattered across the vast Australian landscape. Thus, traditional Aboriginal Dreamings map out the whole human condition on the landscape shaped by the native Australian magical ancestral creators.

Small wonder, then, that the Australian Aboriginal artist, as map-master and interpreter of the cosmos, is a special person in his own society. He is exceptionally in touch with cosmic truth and permitted to encode this in this art. He is a myth-maker. Thus, Bruce Nabekeyo's *Yingarna, the Rainbow Serpent* (1989) eternally recreates the world by swallowing her human offspring and regurgitating them metaphysically into another dimension as features of the landscape;   Maxie Tjampitjinpa's termite queen, a symbol of fertility and reproduction, enjoys her own *Flying Ant Dreaming* (1988), where uncountable earth- and sky-toned dots stand for the creatures' nuptial swarming and mystical acts of creation. Malcolm Jagarra and Maureen Hudson's *Wardapi* (1994) depicts Maureen's mother's Dreaming of the goanna, a creature mythically associated with fertility and healing.

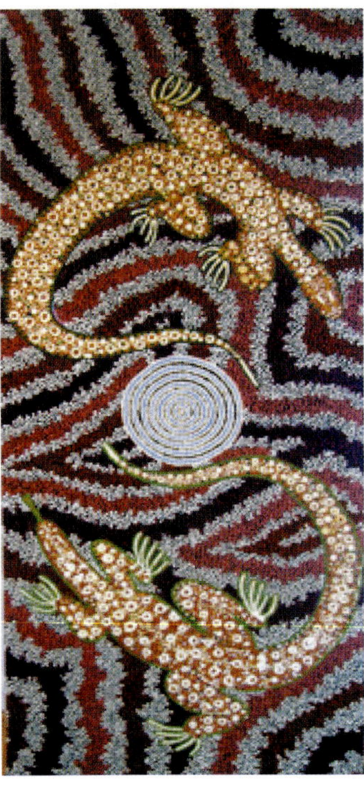

Figure 10: Malcolm Jagarra and Maureen Hudson: *Wardapi* (1994). 144 x 61 cm. Acrylic on canvas. www.aboriginalaustralia.com

The artist commemorates the acts of the supernatural ancestors and charts the land for the Aboriginal past, present and future. He paints the Dreamings for his people and for us. His painting is magical. It has the power to work for good, perhaps encouraging affection or fertility, as it can also work for malevolent purposes, where sorcery is invoked in revenge or retribution and paintings contort human shapes in the belief that this will inflict pain or punishment on the subject.

The art of Aboriginal Australia now enjoys the status of "fine art". Works are displayed not only in ethnographical or anthropological museums as historical records but in art museums and commercial galleries as well. This was by no means always the case. Aboriginal art was first exhibited to the general public in Adelaide, Australia, in the 1880s. The exhibition's title, "Dawn of Art" clearly indicates that its focus was on Australian history or anthropology rather than on the product as a work of artistic imagination. Aboriginal art was shown abroad in the 1940s when the "Art of Australia 1788-1941" exhibit toured the United States and Canada. For decades, Aboriginal art (as fine art rather than history) was neither understood nor accepted by viewers and critics educated in western European traditions. Even as Aboriginal artists started to move from the country into the Australian cities and began to use popular media such as canvas and acrylics instead of or in addition to bark, bones, wood and earth pigments, their themes and styles still failed to fit into accepted norms of what an artwork should look like. Their work was largely ignored until gradually changing conceptions of art in general, a recognition of non-European artistic values and increased interest in indigenous art and culture opened viewers' eyes to the aesthetic merits of Aboriginal art. This movement went hand in hand with the Aborigines' determination to make themselves respected and relevant in Australian society. Progress was slow, however. Although some Australian state galleries joined the Art Gallery of New South Wales in acquiring Aboriginal collections in the 1970s and 1980s, the Australian National Gallery opened in 1981 showing practically no Aboriginal art. Only in the mid-1980s did this art manage to move out of museums into commercial galleries and start to enjoy some commercial success. So it was that Australian art carved out a significant presence for itself in Thailand in the late 1980s and into the 1990s, as we have seen.

Whatever medium the Australian Aboriginal artist chooses to use, be it acrylic on canvas, pigment on earth or hand-hewn chisel on bare rock, the basic elements of his composition will most often be geometrical in organisation. Straight and wavy lines, circles solo or concentric, stripes, diamonds, cross-hatching and fields of dots share the image with shapes from nature to render the artists' Dreamings in dynamic style. These patterns form part of the religious iconography that transforms the mundane surface to which they applied into a mystical and meaningful one. If a painted Dreaming is an encoded cosmic message, its patterns can be interpreted: repeated patterns may represent the ebb and flow of spiritual forces; a series of diamond shapes may stand for fresh streams feeding ancestral lagoons and flowing out down from these into the plains. Dots may be the air-bubbles of air-breathing water creatures – turtles or water snakes. Fields of dots can indicate sparks, fire, burnt ground, smoke, clouds or rain. Shapes may be clear to the casual observer or hidden, visible only to the artist and his initiated public, depending on the level of revelation he desires for a particular painting. Dots may outline an image, fill in distinct fields within the composition or else cover the entire picture surface, as happens in Robert Ambrose Cole's 1994 *Untitled*, where white dots uniformly arranged in squares subdivided into triangular segments fill the whole canvas. The optical effect absorbs the viewer, leading him towards an abstract perception of a higher spirituality. Dots permit no hard and fast interpretation. They may stand for anything from fluffy bird-down to ancient origins in ground painting; they may indicate differences in topography and vegetation; overlaying other dots or different patterns, they may mask secrets or herald a spiritual presence.

Most strikingly, perhaps, dots add movement, shine and brilliance to the artist's work. This can mean the radiance that indicates the presence of a supernatural power or, when applied to sculptured women's bodies, the warmth of their health, beauty and fertility. Dots visually add brightness and shimmer to a work. Background dots can convey sparkling water, rainbows, dappled sunlight on woodland's grassy floor. Shininess transforms a dull surface to a state of shimmering brilliance. Brilliance transforms the mundane human condition into a more intense spirituality. Dots are an essential medium of the Aboriginal Australian expression of processes like these.

And Kitti Narod's paintings are a festival of dots. Dots arranged in geometric forms – triangles, squares, lines, stripes and zigzags – frame an image that is again delineated in dots and filled in with systematically grouped and colour-coded dots against a general background of flowers, foliage, mountains, suns and moons composed of dots in every imaginable composition and colour combination. None of this is random. The effect is never overwhelming or confusing.   The whole is so thoughtfully and meticulously brought together that chaos is never a concept that springs to mind. Let's take a look at Kitti's study in staring, *Family* (2005).

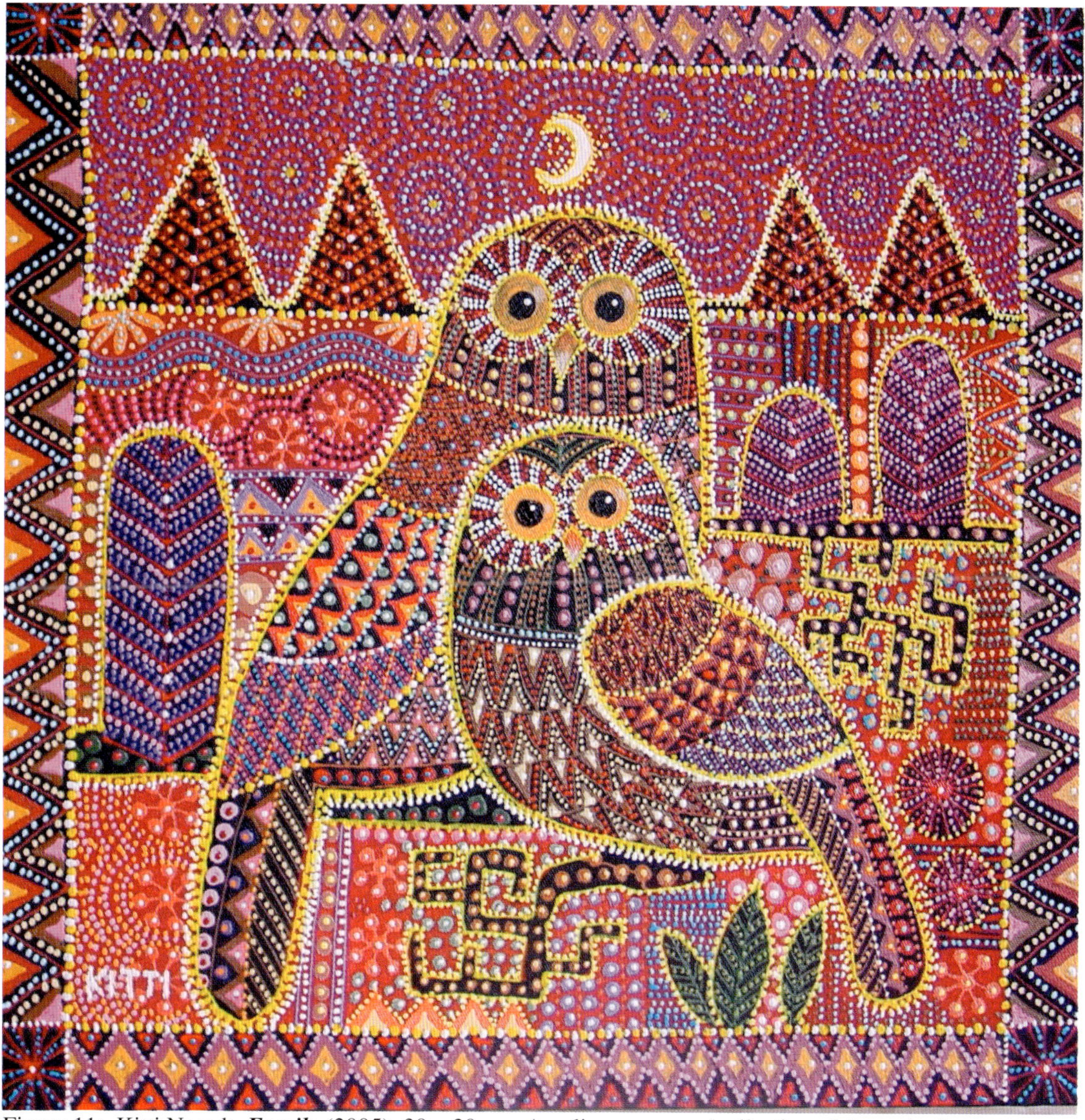

Figure 11: Kitti Narod: *Family* (2005). 30 x 30 cm. Acrylic on canvas (collection of the author).

Leaving aside the "who's going to have to blink first" competition that the owl family has entered into with the observer, notice the painted border at the canvas edges: dotted diamonds at top and bottom, each inlaid with a two-colour diamond-within-a-diamond design centred on a white dot; interlocking two-colour triangles at the sides, separated by a double row of dots, blue and yellow, divided by solid lines; at each corner, a dot-and-line stylised flower or star design, where blue stands out as centred on the pale dot in the middle of each corner square. As a background to the birds, variously sized dotted fields, mainly vaguely rectangular or square in delineation, where dots in pinks, purples, blues and yellows arranged in curved or wavy lines, triangles, circles or pinwheels serve as a backdrop to trees, mountains (or are they conifers?), twisted branches and a central crescent moon, shining solid white outlined in brilliant dotted yellow. This is night-time, but it is no less bright than the sunniest of days. The "family" here is closeness, owl cuddled on the chest of owl, and warmth.

Warmth and vitality are characteristic of Kitti Narod's work. A young painter working in a stridently urban environment, Kitti is close to nature. Maybe the latent animism and Buddhist empathy for all created things that underlie the Thai sensibility are strong in Kitti as they are, within the Australian context, in his aboriginal confederates. Kitti's painting is not socially or politically engaged. We do not read an alienated, tormented soul into, or out of, his work. The spiritual presence his painting exudes is joyful and inspires joy in the viewer.   His work, far from being flat, dull or even merely amusing or decorative, is intriguing and associative, never dreary or disturbing. How appropriate that Kitti Narod should express this spirituality in an Aboriginal pictorial idiom, tapping into the native Australians' closeness to a metaphysical world from which originates our own. Kitti's dots, more versatile colourwise than those of the Australian works, are groupable into an endless variety of shapes, patterns and alignments so that, when you add the available colour permutations, it becomes clear that Kitti's possibilities are virtually infinite. And that's not the end of it. Dots on top of other dots rank high on Kitti's stylistic menu. Kitti's layering dots upon dots adds visual depth and texture to his canvas, rather as Aboriginal layering of geometric designs covers secret meanings for them with more public signs suitable for general viewing. Our close-up (below) shows an example of Kitti's dots in action.

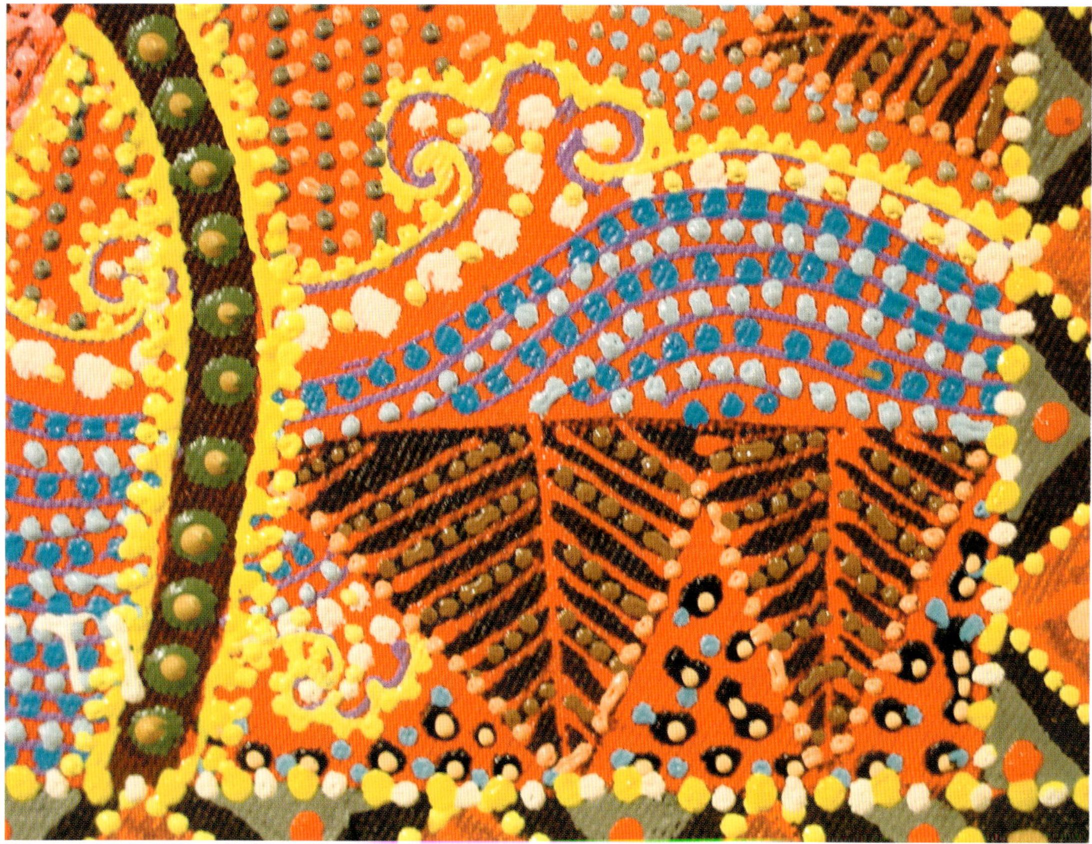

Figure 12: Kitti Narod: *Two Lotus* (2005). 50 x 50 cm. Acrylic on canvas (detail).

The overall effect of Kitti's dot paintings is one of smoothness. Viewers who stand well away from his paintings to look at the overall effect often ask what they are made of. People think they may be painted ceramic, minute mosaics, beads or embroidery. This is not inappropriate, given Kitti's liking for mosaics and the Thai genius for textiles and richly embroidered wall-hangings. Baffled observers are drawn closer and closer to the paintings until they can see the smooth dots clearly against the ground colour. Even then, many run their fingers gently over the canvas, just to make sure in a tactile way that their eyes are not deceiving them. What a wonderful testimonial this is to Kitti's artistry. He draws the viewer ever closer into contact with his work, absorbing the observer into his artistic world as the viewer absorbs Kitti's imagination into his own.

Contact is key to an understanding of Kitti's art. Where Kitti overpaints the side edges of his chunky canvases with dot designs, this further dimension to his painted frame makes contact between the face of the painting and the wall on which it hangs, integrating the artwork into its environment.

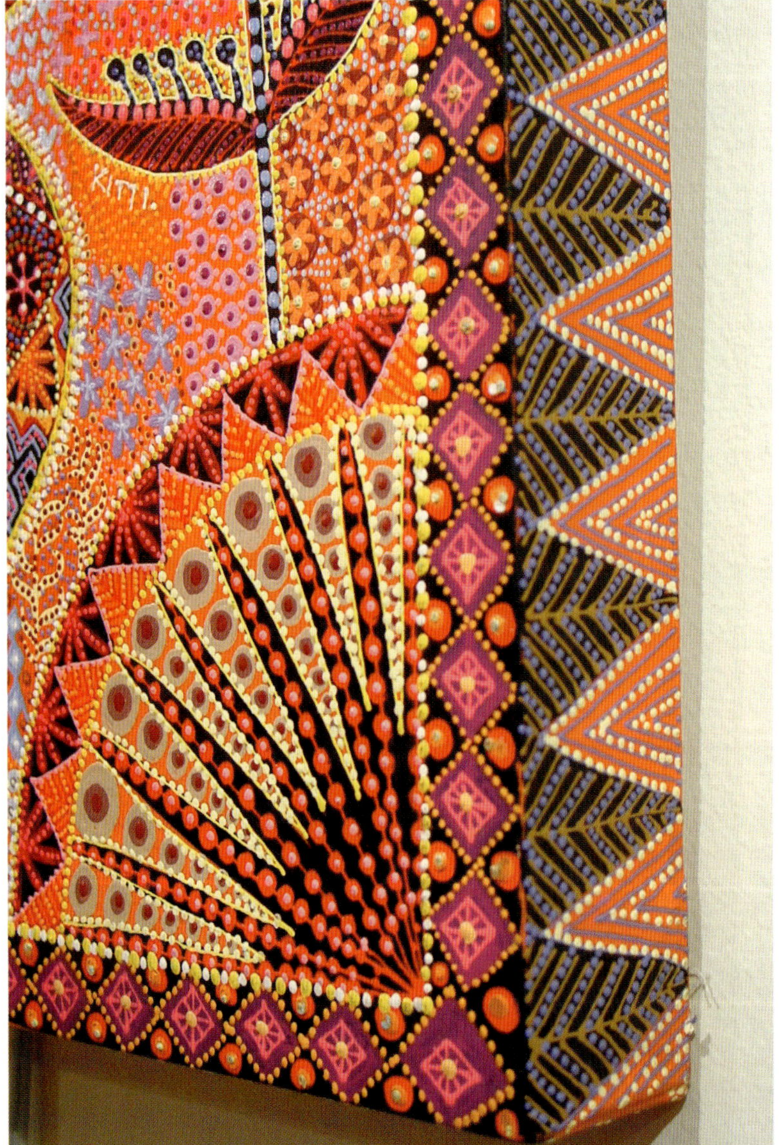

Figure 13: Kitti Narod: *Termite Queen* (2005). 50 x 50 cm. Acrylic on canvas (detail)

Designs and geometrics are closely compacted within Kitti's pictures to create his own textured designs, the details of which are appreciated only with closer viewing, when the observer stands right in front of the canvas. How Kitti achieves clarity and order within a close configuration of shapes and colours and how he applies his paint without designs and colours impinging on each other are the artist's own closely guarded secrets.

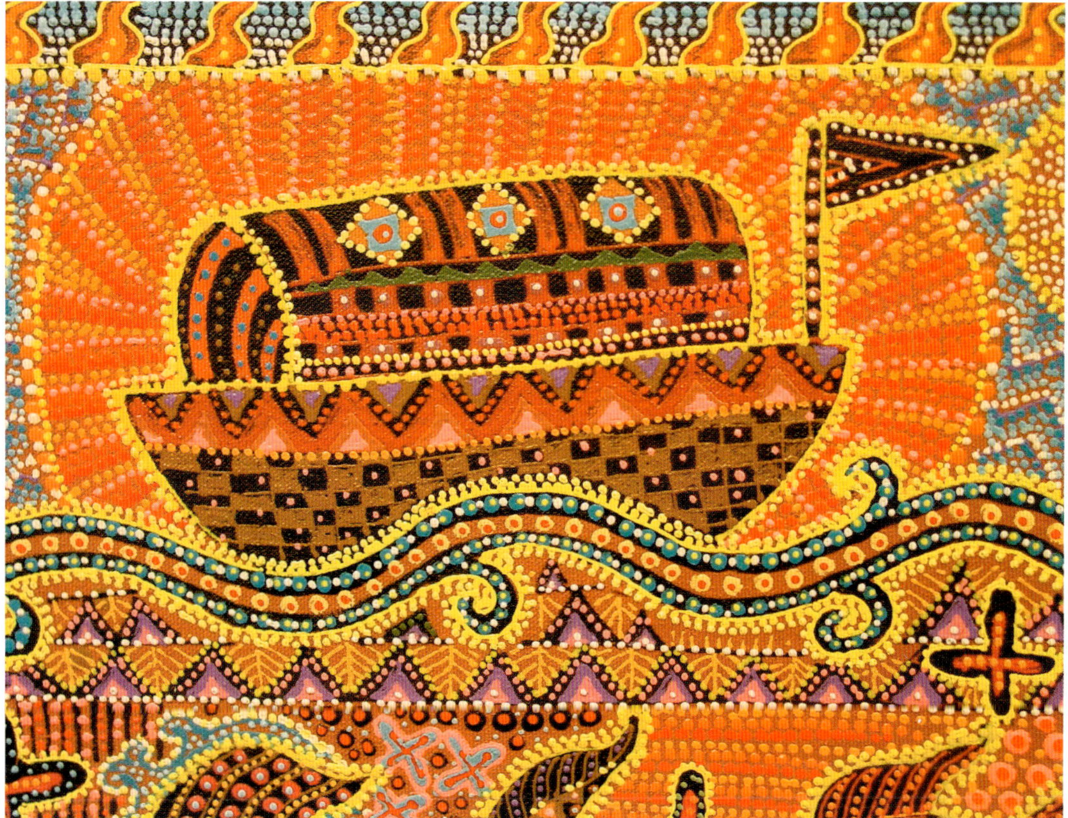

Figure 14: Kitti Narod: *Destine* (2005). 30 x 30 cm. Acrylic on canvas. (Detail).

Kitti's **Destine**, for example, combines a wealth of colour and design within a few square inches of canvas, but clarity is maintained, untainted by any visual or conceptual confusion. At the same time, Kitti's composition is radiant and dynamic as the boat illuminated by a halo of light tosses on restless waves.

Composition enhances closeness in **Family**, where a strong verticality unites owls and moon. Imagine a straight vertical line cutting down through the Moon's crescent and straight towards the bottom of the picture through the owls' faces, between the two sets of unflinchingly staring eyes and through the yellow pointed beaks. As the owls' gaze transfixes the viewer, so the birds are transfixed by their immobility, two bodies close and comfortable together.

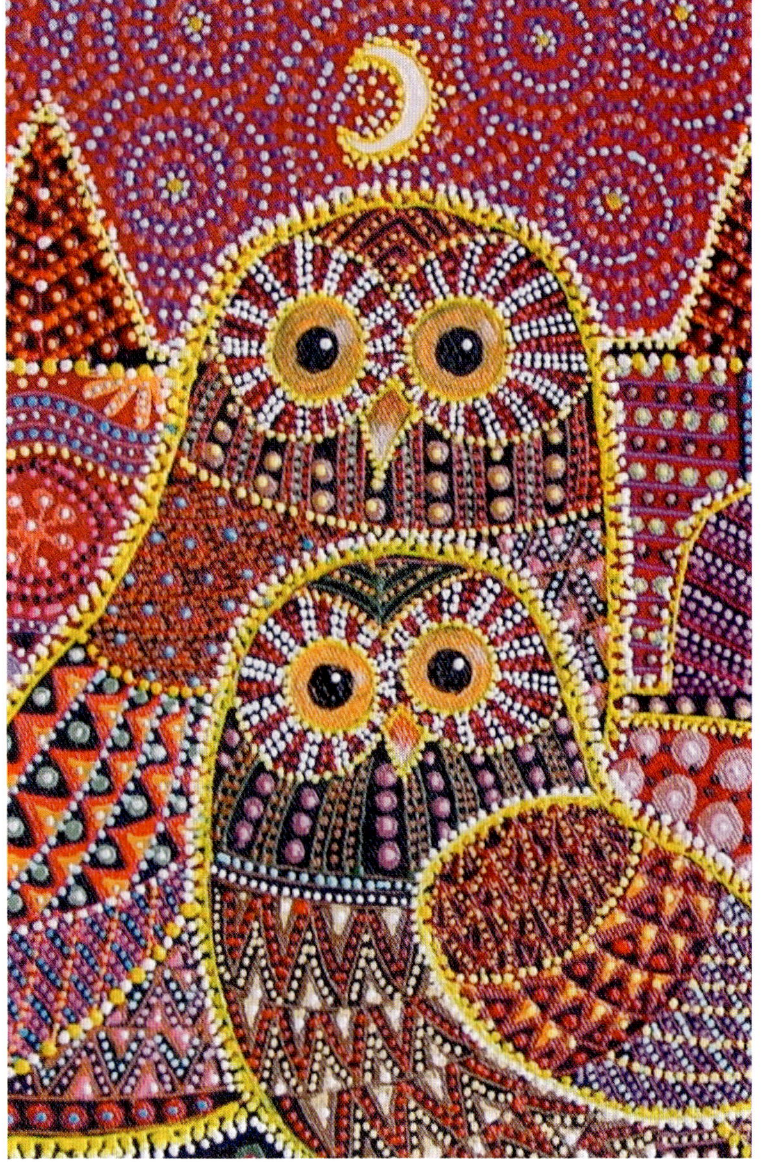

Figure 15: Kitti Narod: *Family* (detail).

It is said that Australian Aboriginal mythology believes that bats are the souls of men and owls the souls of women. Hence, owls are sacred creatures, "your sister is an owl – and the owl is your sister" (www.owlpages.com). These creatures of the night are frequently associated with magic and mystery. Indian mythology is particularly strong in owl lore. Is there a message for us in the gaze of Narod's owl family? Rest assured, there's no bad news here. Narod's tranquil starry sky and ordered landscape are proof enough of that.

Kitti's ***Couple*** conveys a closeness of another kind.   Humans generally prefer to keep their sex acts private, but the animal kingdom is quite another matter. Where Kitti's owls exude a confident serenity perhaps born of what we would look upon as nice behaviour, his frogs here glow with a passion that is all too anthropomorphically mirrored in the expressions on their faces.

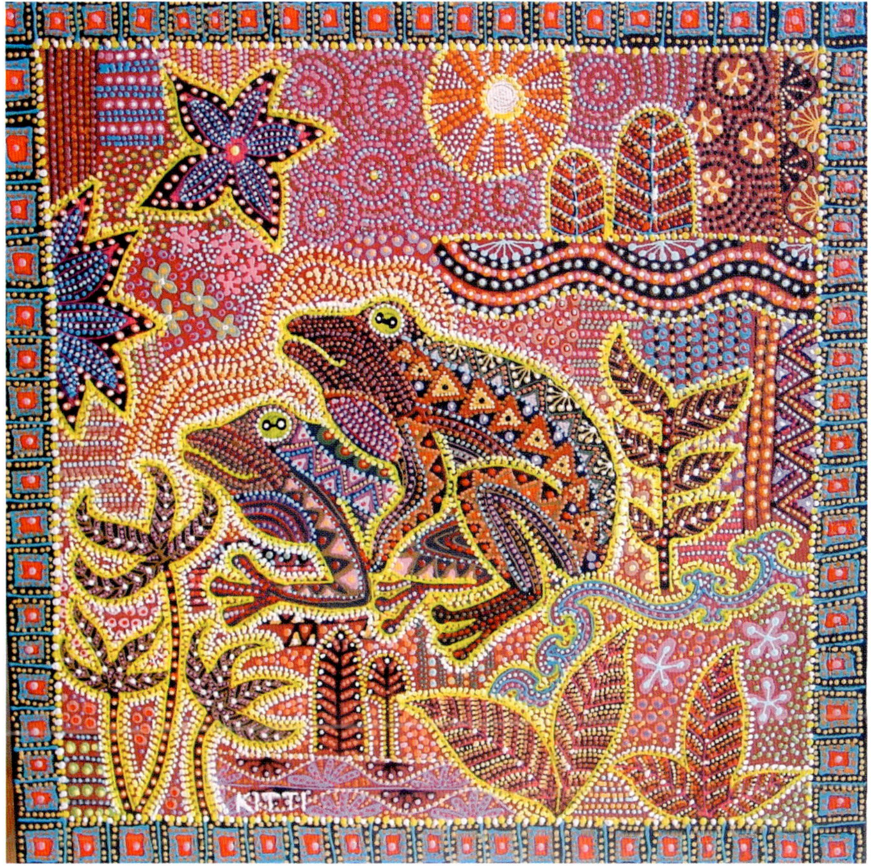

Figure 16: Kitti Narod: ***Couple*** (2005). 30 x 30. Acrylic on canvas.

Frogs and toads are mythically associated with fertility in many cultures. Ancient China saw the toad as a predominantly passive female force ("yin"), as opposed to the positive, male "yang". Ancient Egypt saw frogs as the symbol of fertility, water, renewal and birth. In pre-Columbian South and Central America, frogs and toads are mythologically associated with rainfall, fertility and childbirth. Frogs and toads transform from egg to tadpole to adult animal. Many cultures thus associate them with creation and re-creations, and with the magical secrets of transformations. European folk-legends and fairytales involve frogs in mystery, trickery, transformation, love and sex. When is a frog not a frog? Kiss the horrible frog and he will turn into a handsome prince and whisk you away to a life of "happy ever after", girls may be told in fairytales. And it is often but a short hop from a kiss to copulation. No wonder Kitti's frogs exude radiance. There's more to them than meets the eye.

Close encounters are not always cosy or copulative, however. Kitti Narod's **Conflict** sets two rather wolf-like dogs practically nose to nose in a snarling, slavering face-off over what looks to be a somewhat insignificant bowl of water. The viewer is captivated by the tension that locks these animals in the moments before battle breaks out.

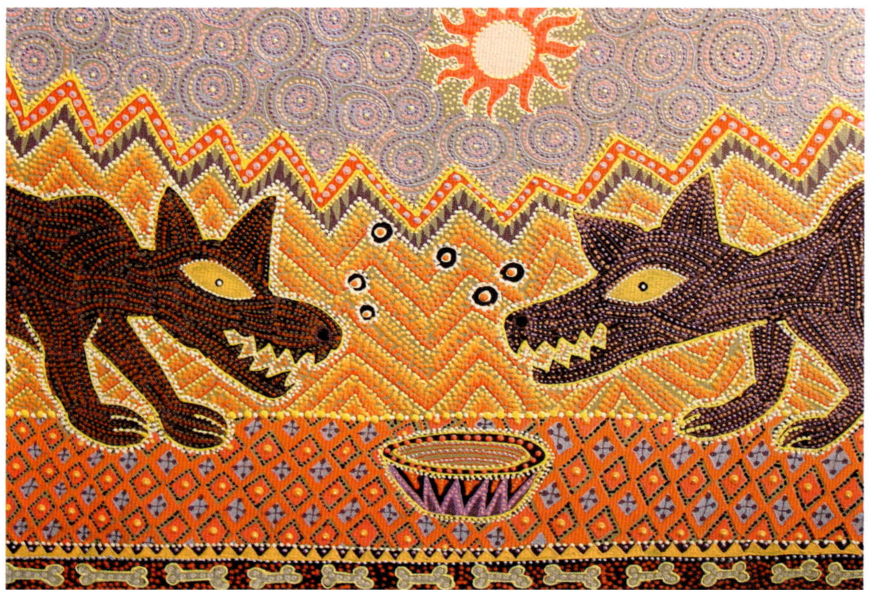

Figure 17: Kitti Narod: **Conflict** (2005). 72 x 32.5 cm. Acrylic on canvas. (Detail).

Curiously, Kitti's dot technique acquires a cartoon-like quality here: notice the staring eyes and bared fangs that so typically stand for animal rivalry and aggression; six central bubbles speak of snuffling and snorting and spumes of spit; the sun beating down on the animals, exacerbating their thirst, is a child's sun drawing, not like the suns that feature in so many of Kitti's paintings; and dog-bones in caricature, like the dog-bone treats we buy for our pets, rim the canvas humorously, perhaps in mockery of the exaggerated attitudes assumed by the two animals. Despite their intensity and despite the blistering heat exuded by Narod's colour scheme and the zigzag waves of warmth rising from the ground in response to the burning sun, these animals are foolish. Ironically, the dogs are very alike, practically identical in size, colour and shape. They could be brothers. Their bowl is small, but sharing its contents could slake the thirst of both in harmony, whereas the pitched battle that is about to break out between them will almost certainly spill the water, leaving both dogs even thirstier than before

22

and perhaps even bleeding, maimed or worse as a result of the fight. There is no serenity here, no understanding, respect or any other civilised quality. Of course, these are just dogs … or are they? How often do men, women and nation-states conflict as ferociously as these creatures, with little but loss and destruction to show for it in the end.

Kitti Narod's dogs stand still, poised instants before a furious battle breaks out between them. Hostility in **Enemy**, however, whirls in a circular fury of flying feathers. Bred to show no mercy, this pair of fighting cocks is here locked in an unforgiving dance of death.

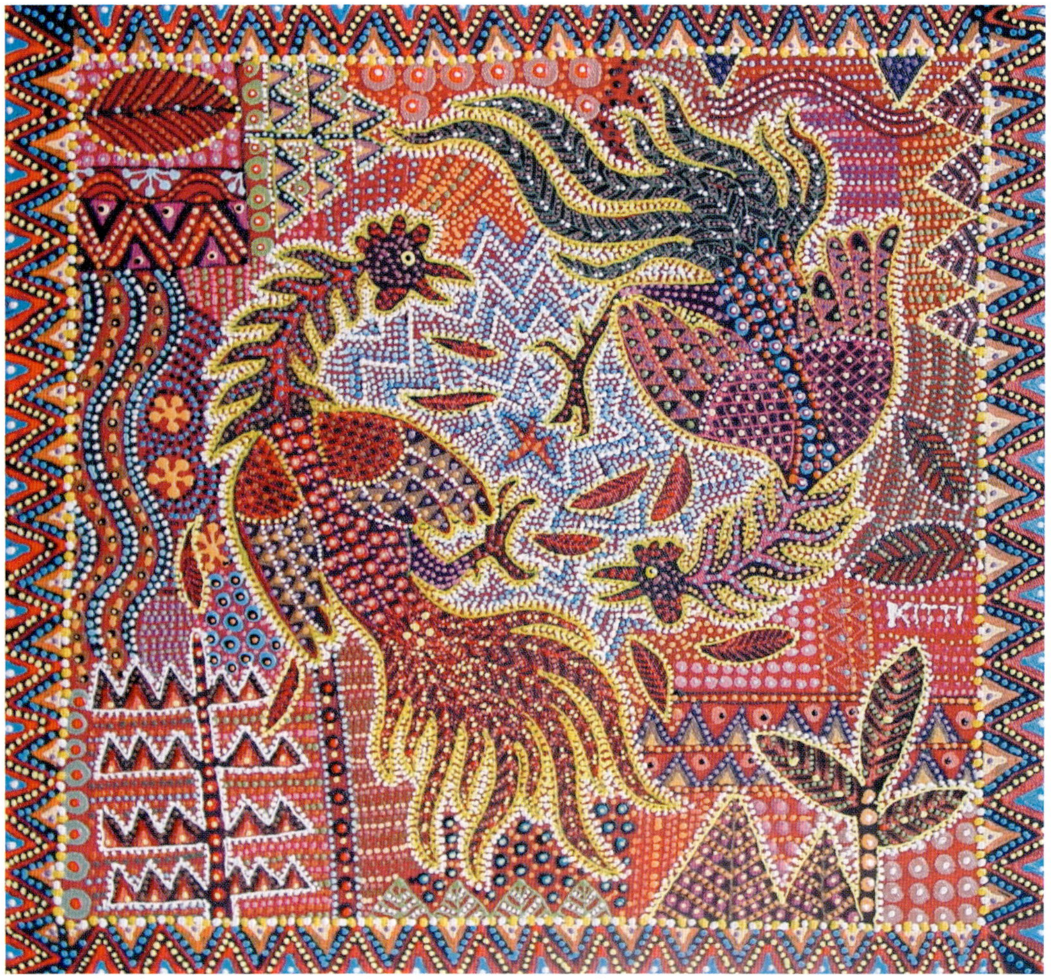

Figure 18: Kitti Narod: **Enemy** (2005). 30 x 30 cm. Acrylic on canvas. (Private collection)

This canvas is packed with detail. Sharp-pointed triangular shapes abound, from the painted on-canvas frame to the tree-like detail at the bottom left and the occasional claw-like outcroppings that threaten the central figures from the inner line of the picture's painted border. Beaks, gasping and grasping for the enemy, scrawny, feathered, stretching necks, claws so nearly making contact within a flurry of zigzag star shapes, and those staring, desperate eyes: every detail expresses aggression, hatred and death. Those of us unused to cock-fighting would like to free these

24

cockerels, but the Buddhist Wheel of Life and Death, known also as the Wheel of Law, symbolises passion, one of the three cardinal sins, in the shape of the cock. So there is no escaping their destiny: our cockerels are born to fight with a passion and die as they do so. Not always entirely in vain, however. Thai history reveres Prince Naresuan's victorious fighting cock as symbolic of the nation's eventual victory in her on-going territorial contests with the neighbouring Burmese. This tale from the ancient time when Ayutthaya was the nation's capital enhances the fighting cock's relevance within Thai folk mythology, as does Kitti Narod's ***Enemy*** even today.

Many of Narod's paintings engage his animal protagonists in a dynamic circular movement. The circle, or wheel, is a fundamental feature of the Buddhist culture. The Wheel of Life, or Wheel of Law, depicts the cyclical nature of life according to Buddhism, where life, death and infinite reincarnations precede the attainment of Nirvana, or the heavenly escape from materialism and earthly sufferings.

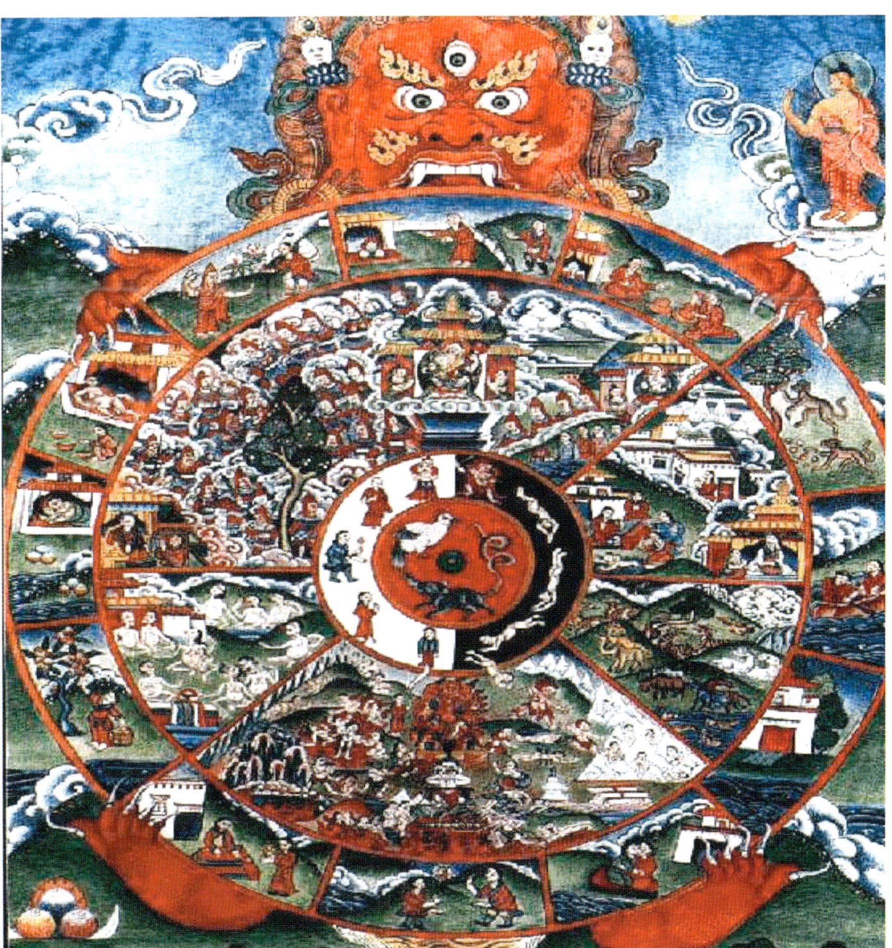

Figure 19: Tibetan style Buddhist mandala: ***The Wheel of Life and Death***. www.bhuddanet.net

A mandala like the one depicted in Figure 19 may be used to aid meditation or help disciples understand the Buddhist concepts of karma and rebirth. Often painted in tiny, intricate detail, mandalas may depict the Buddha's Four Truths – the existence of earthly suffering, its origin and cause, the ending or prevention of suffering and the practices that allow us to free ourselves from suffering – as well as the sins that bring on suffering and the fate that befalls sinners and the less than sinful. The notion of this wheel may date from the lifetime of the Buddha himself, and similar notions are current in many other faiths. Mediaeval European art and literature, for instance, may symbolise life's cycle as a wheel, rising from birth to the height of a person's power and achievements, declining then to death or ignominy. How many are raised by the wheel of fortune to dizzying heights, only to tumble and be crushed then beneath it as others are raised high in their turn.

Kitti Narod's painted creatures, however, leaving his fighting cockerels aside, generally gyrate in a wholesome whirl of positive proportions. What could be more inviting, for example, than a Pacific party? In the detail below, all manner of water creatures have joined the dance.

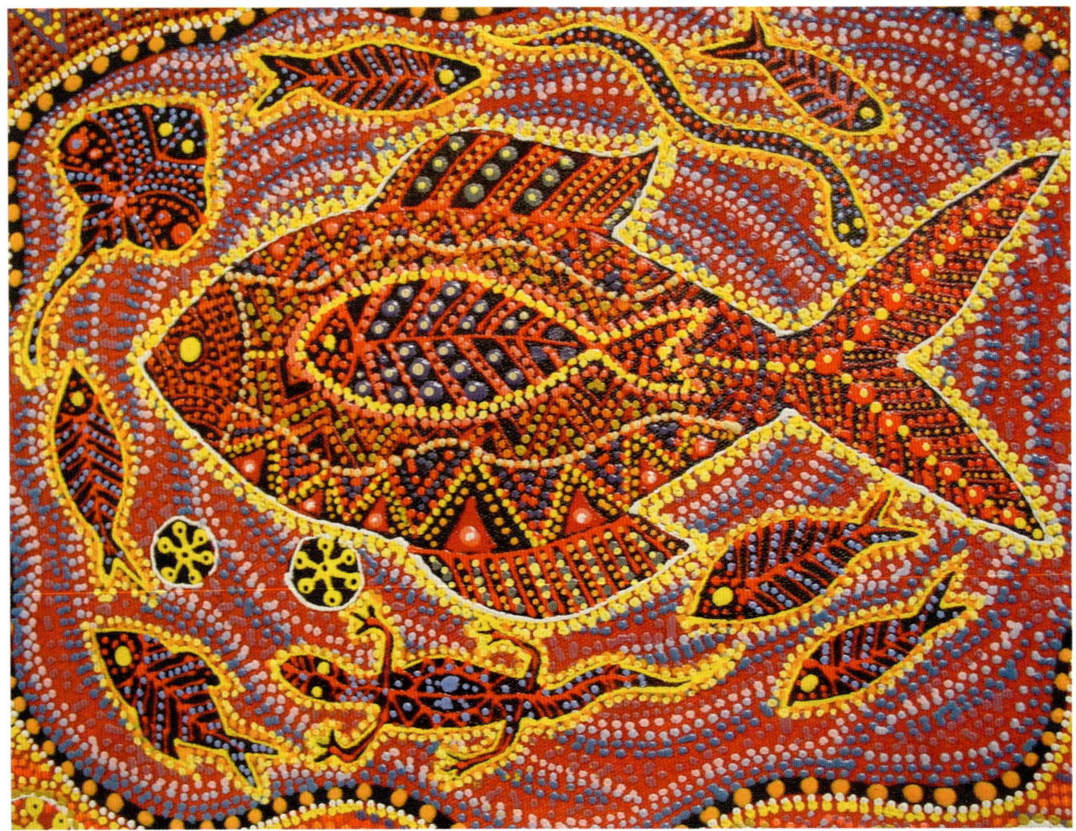

Figure 20: Kitti Narod: *Pacific Party* (detail).

They whirl in unison, these lizards, snakes, starfish, rays and fish within other fish, to the music of dots on dots in sizes great and small. Where the party scene is encircled by a defining band of yellow dots on a darker ground, triangular shapes at both sides perhaps stand for shore-lines, whilst waves roll above the revellers beneath a bright, tropical sun, and the sea-bed is dotted with anemones and starfish. Most strangely, hybrid verticals, seemingly part fish, part plant, stand to either side of sun and sky. We will be looking at these mysteries again later, as they reappear in Kitti's *Evolution*.

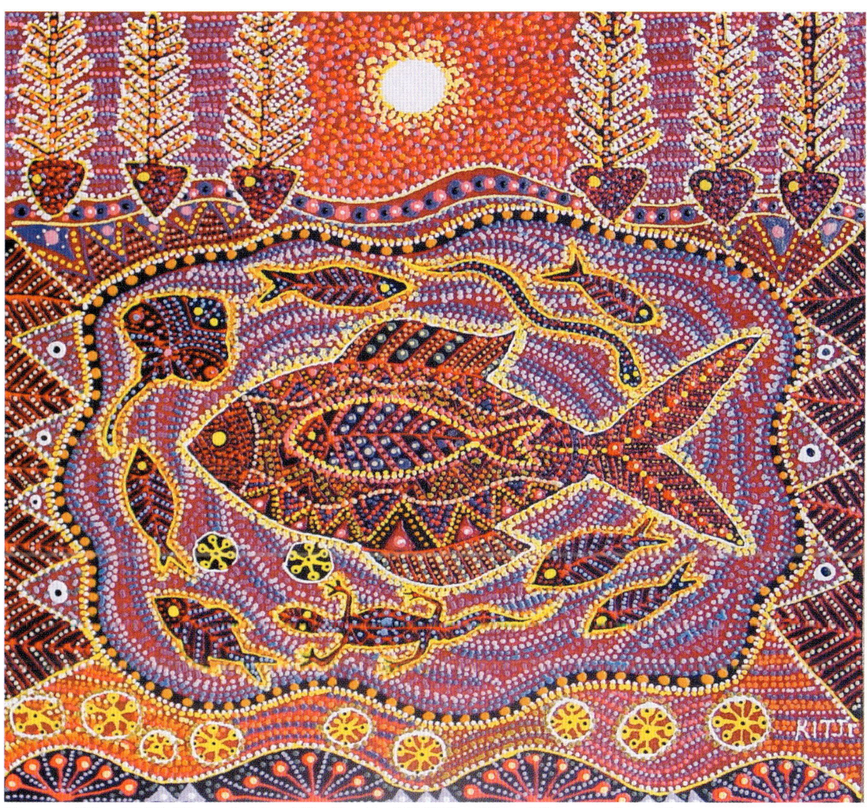

Figure 21: Kitti Narod: *Pacific Party* (2005). 30 x 30 cm. Acrylic on canvas.

Kitti's Pacific partygoers are laden with metaphorical meaning. We recall the Australian aboriginal Rainbow Serpent, a creator of their ancestral landscape, while the goanna, a terrestrial cousin of Narod's swimming lizard, brings to mind Jagarra and Hudson's *Wardapi*, a symbol of fertility and healing. The indigenous astronomers of Arnhem Land in northern Australia named the stars they saw in their vast night sky after the animals with which they shared their continent. For them, the constellation of the

Southern Cross, so prominent in the Australian Night sky, is a stingray chased by a shark.

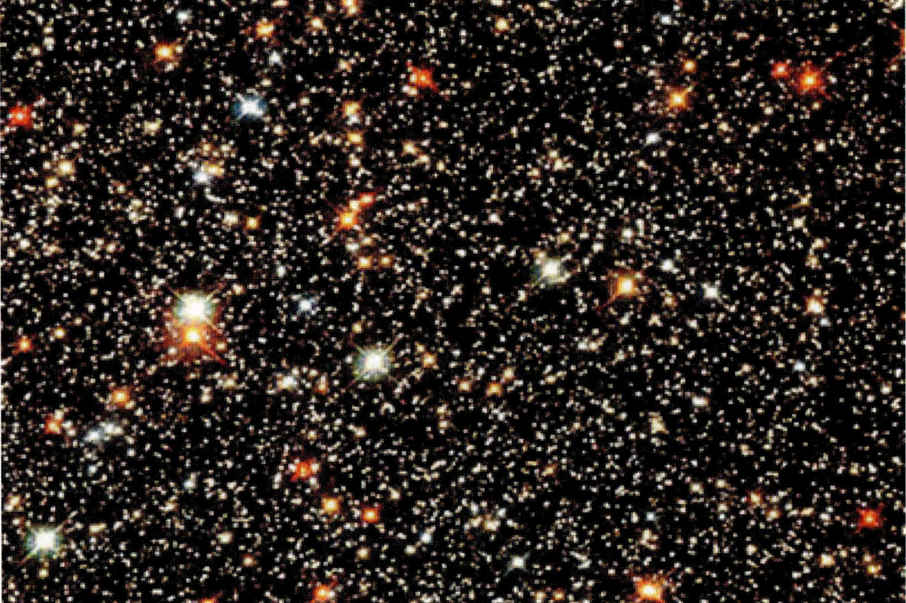

Figure 22: The Southern Cross Constellation in the Australian night sky.   www.abc.net.au. 16-8-2005

Astrophysicists are currently investigating the Aborigines' rich cosmic mythology as an aid to understanding how different peoples all over the world understand their universe. Let it come as no surprise to us, then, that Kitti Narod's own *Ray* is central to a swimming circle of creatures from the wheel of life, death and rebirth.

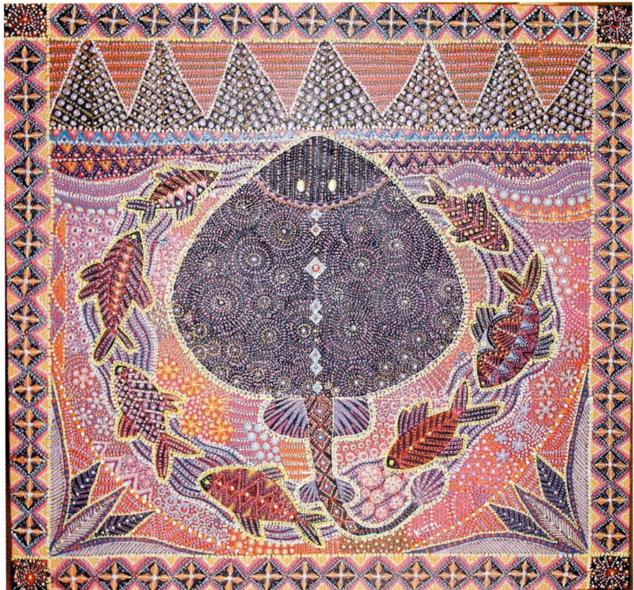

Figure 23: Kitti Narod: *Ray* (2005). 50 x 50 cm. Acrylic on canvas. (Private collection)

28

Birds, fish, rays, reptiles, creepy-crawlies and the occasional dog abound in Kitti Narod's paintings. Human figures, however, do not. Kitti's Buddha faces are the exception to this norm. We recall that Thai painting traditionally did not deal with representative human figures or portraits, whilst Buddha statuary, on the other hand, dominated art and architecture for centuries. The Lord Buddha himself stressed during his lifetime that, even upon attaining Enlightenment, he was no more than a human being and did not want to be regarded or revered as a god. Despite the fact that he is of course now revered perhaps more than he would have liked, it is, therefore, legitimate to consider representations of the Buddha as human figures, albeit with mystical content and meaning. In early 2005, Kitti Narod attempted a series of Buddha paintings in his adapted Aboriginal dot technique. All these paintings exhibit a certain tension between the serenity of the Buddha and the dynamic of the natural phenomena that surround him. *Two Lotus* is perhaps one of Kitti's more successful combinations of the spiritual and natural spheres of existence. The painting enjoys a satisfying balance between the mystical and the material world.

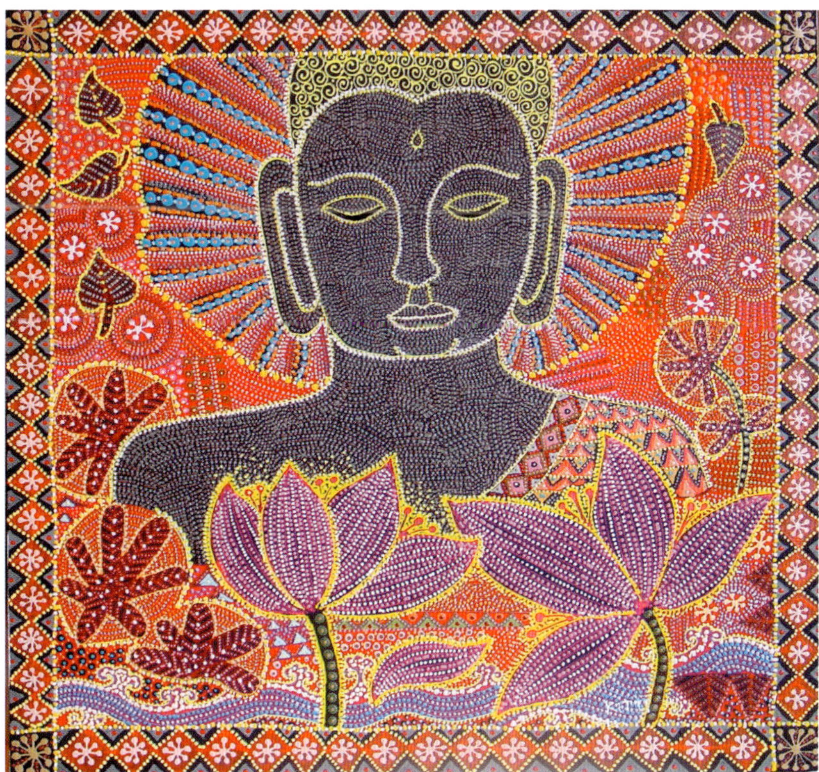

Figure 24: Kitti Narod: *Two Lotus* (2005). 30 x 30 cm. Acrylic on canvas.

The Buddha's gaze is characteristically lowered in contemplation of the inner self rather than the outside world. His skin is dark, his head and features radiant in the lightly outlined halo that is common to both Christian and Chinese iconography. Holy bodhi leaves and white blossoms drift gently over a warm, textured ground. Two lotus flowers rise up out of the moving water in the lower field, blossoming for their Buddha. The painted frame around the canvas is a coherent diamond design with stylised florals in each corner. There is no contest here between inner and outer worlds, between meditation and nature.

In **Buddha** (Figure 25), a similarly drawn Buddha head dominates the canvas. The eyes here are open to the world, the gaze still lowered in contemplation and humility. Lotus blossoms are reduced, the single bodhi leaf is uncomfortably close to the Buddha's brow. Dark tones predominate. The natural world is peripheral, cramped towards the edges of the painting.

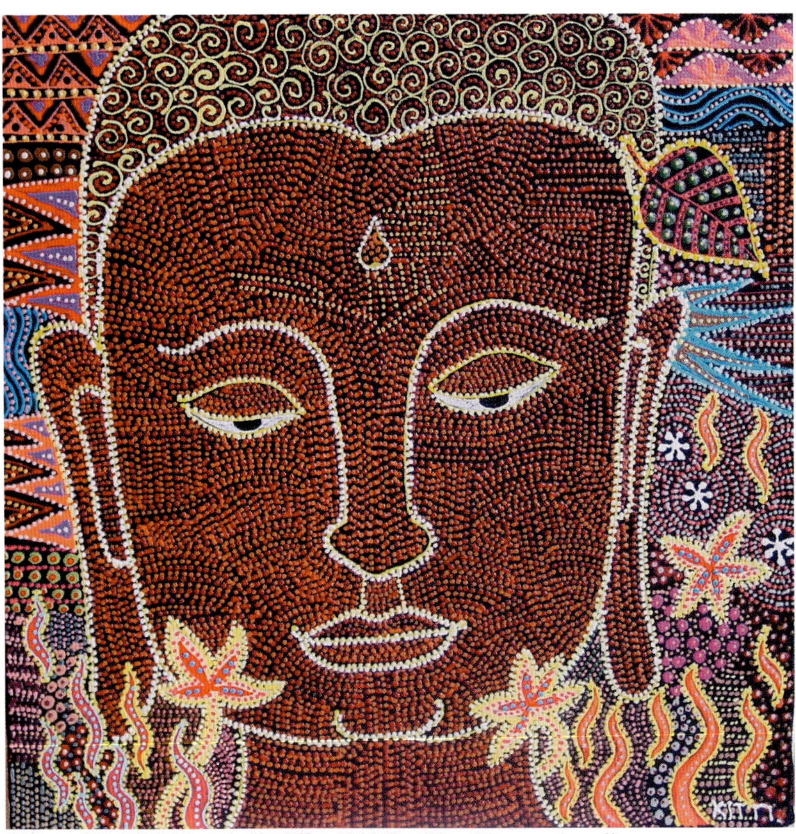

Figure 25: Kitti Narod: **Buddha** (2005). 30 x 30 cm. Acrylic on canvas.

30

The artist has confessed that he was not comfortable painting the Buddha, which he did on request, not entirely happy with the way things turned out. In *Nirvana Land III,* the Buddha's face, uncharacteristically in profile this time, turns towards the natural world and is almost crowded out of the picture by it.

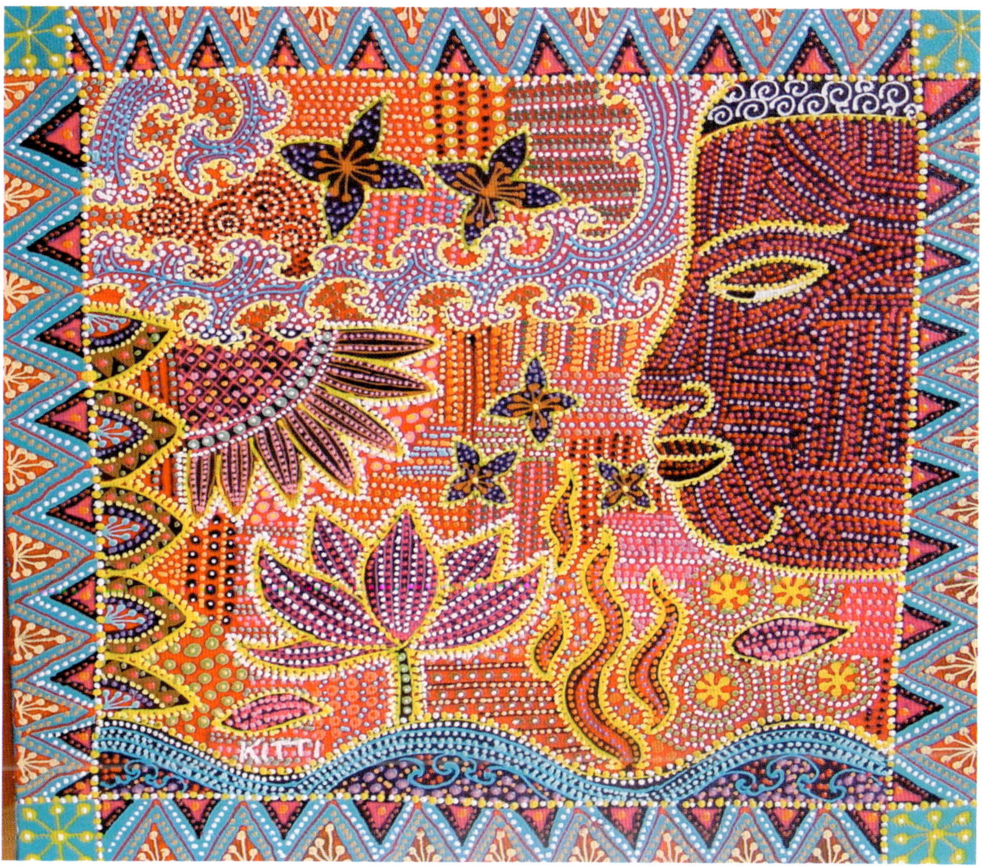
Figure 26: Kitti Narod: *Nirvana Land III* (2005). 30 x 30 cm. Acrylic on canvas.

There is a reason for this, however. Fire, wind and water, the lotus, the sun/sunflower centre left and the predominantly linear background pattern here tell us that the contemplative gaze of Kitti's Buddha far from negates the myriad attractions·of the material world of nature. Inner peace seeks serenity now, but *Nirvana Land III* seems to cry out for serenity "not yet" – the world we and Kitti live in is still too bouncy and buoyant, too attractively agitated for us to want to abandon it just yet. An attachment to the material world may be a stumbling block to the attainment of Nirvana, but Kitti's paintings reveal, whether he wants them to or not, just how much he enjoys materiality, especially when the world is as bright and joyous as he depicts it. Kitti's Buddha's blessing here confirms the value of the natural world. Buddhist teaching might hold Nirvana and freedom from materiality to be the highest form of heaven, but we are encouraged also to find joy in the material world as we pass through it. This is no bad thing, if you consider that millennia of reincarnations into the material world are required before anything approaching Nirvana can be attained!

Charles Darwin's revolutionary notion of the "survival of the fittest", often erroneously interpreted to justify strong-arm policies where "fit" is taken to mean "powerful", seminally told the shocked nineteenth century that the only creatures to survive long-tcrm are those which can evolve to "fit" best into their environment. This includes human beings. Evolution is thus the process by which creatures adapt to their changing surroundings: flexible species that fit in live on; misfits die out.

Artists, too, may evolve. Pablo Picasso's long career exemplifies the many thematic and stylistic variations that can be developed by a single artist. Kitti Narod still stands at the start of his artistic career, but his art is by no means at a standstill.   We can already trace some development in his art and should suspect that his imagination allows for unforeseen future changes.

Kitti's flowers and foliage compositions are particularly successful. A comparison of some of his 2004 production with that of the first part of 2005 shows that similar elements recur frequently. ***Bounty*** (2004), for example, or ***Foliage,*** of the same year, juxtapose single, broad-leafed verticals with vertical tree shapes bearing a number of smaller leaves; the sun tends to shine from the upper left-hand quadrant of the canvas; there is no painted border; elements tend to congregate in roughly rectangular blocks.

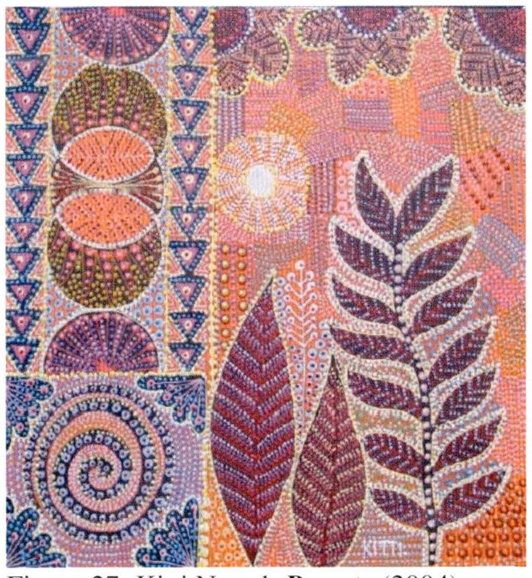

Figure 27: Kitti Narod: ***Bounty*** (2004).
30 x 30 cm. Acrylic on canvas. (Private collection).

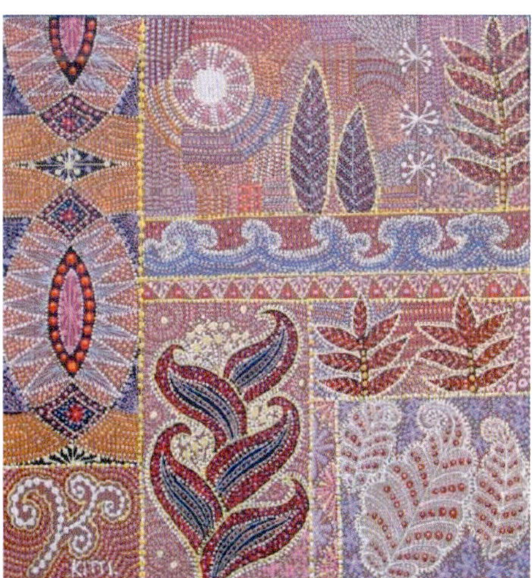

Figure 28: Kitti Narod: ***Foliage*** (2004).
 30 x 30 cm. Acrylic on canvas. (Private Collection).

Kitti's ***Sundance*** series of 2005 echoes many of these themes, with the exception that the format is larger and, where the 2004 paintings stress pink and lilac tones, the ***Sundance*** series works more intensely with reds and oranges.

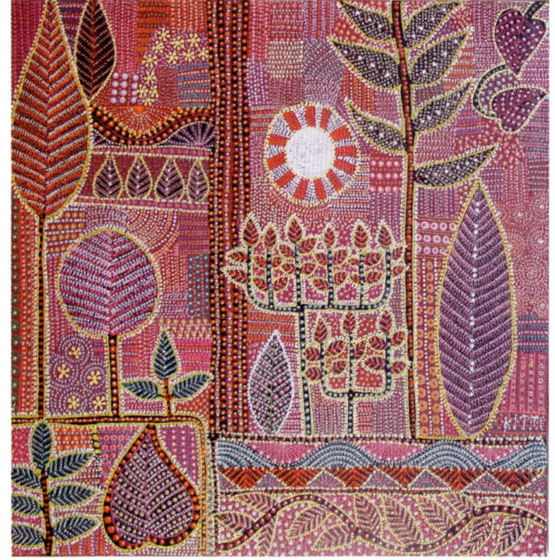

Figure 29: Kitti Narod: ***Sundance I*** (2005).
50 x 50 cm. Acrylic on canvas.

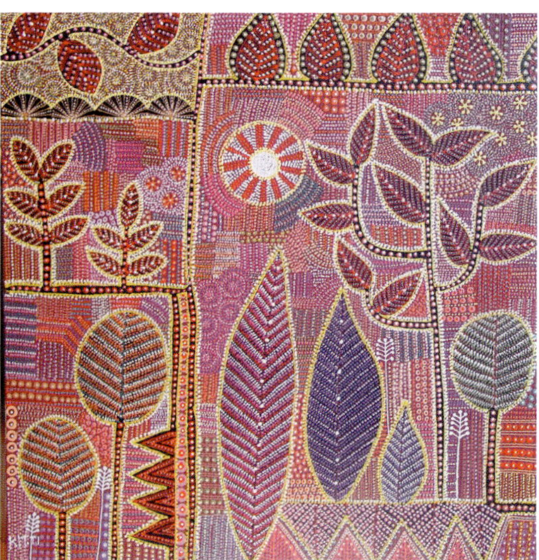

Figure 30: Kitti Narod: ***Sundance II*** (2005)
50 x 50 cm. Acrylic on canvas.

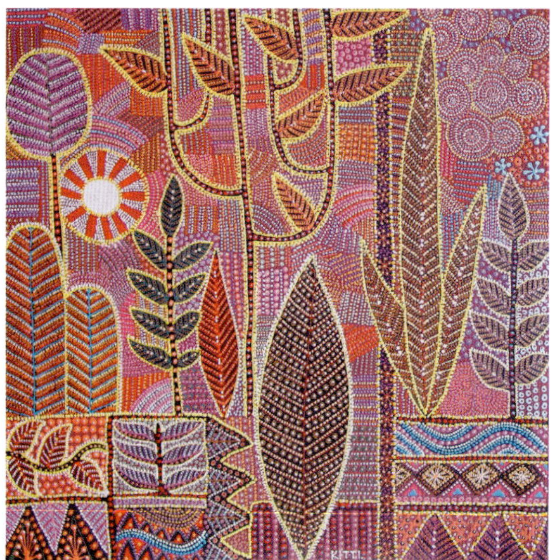

Figure 31: Kitti Narod: ***Sundance III*** (2005).
50 x 50 cm. Acrylic on canvas.

Reds and oranges in fact predominate in Kitti's work in the first part of 2005. Figure 32 shows in close-up how the **Two Lotus** dot designs are worked on a red base colour. This unobtrusive shift in colour focus will be

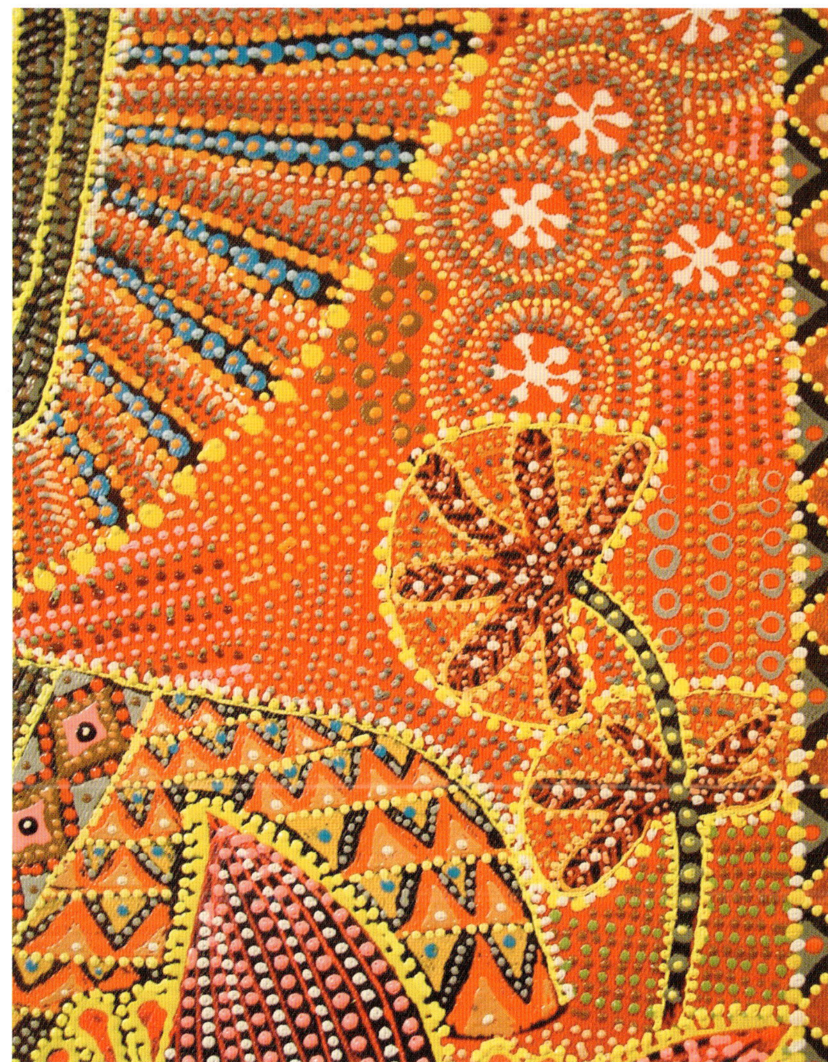

Figure 32: Kitti Narod: **Two Lotus** (detail).

paralleled also by very striking stylistic developments in Narod's work during 2005, as we shall see later.

The notions of development versus extinction are developed in two of Kitti Narod's 2005 dot paintings: ***Evolution*** and ***Happened and Gone.***

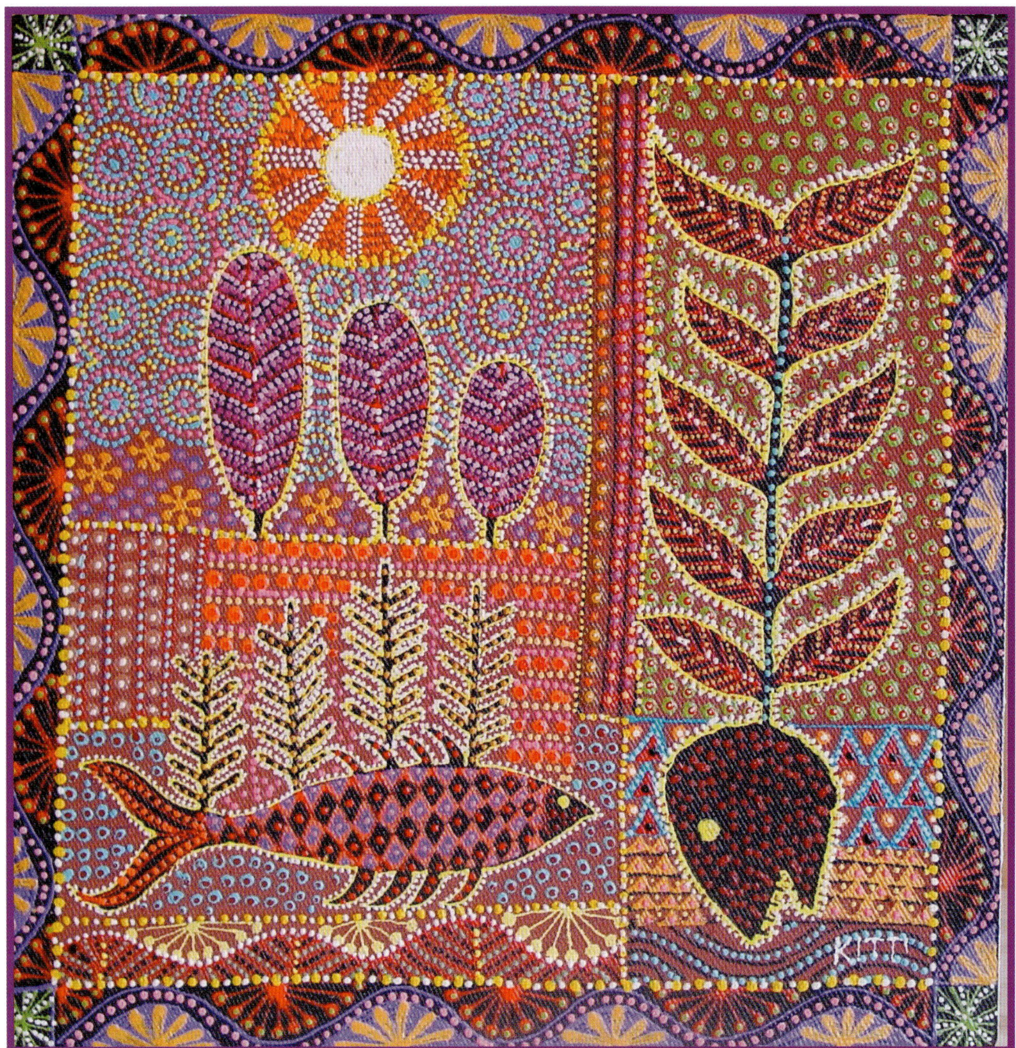

Figure 33: Kitti Narod: *Evolution* (2005). 30 x 30 cm. Acrylic on canvas.

Evolution again features the strange plant/fish hybrid forms we encountered in ***Pacific Party.*** The fish-head/root-ball, topped by the fish-bones/stem-and-leaves formation, vertically dominates the whole right hand side of this canvas, whilst the more recognisable fish swimming bottom left, below a sun-filled landscape, curiously sprouts leafy fronds from its back. The composition blocks off the different elements in rough squares and rectangles, whereas sinuous movement is reserved for the painted border and the concentric circles of the sunlit sky. There is a feeling of stillness to the picture. Evolution is a slow process. Slow, perhaps, but necessary, the

36

alternative to evolution being extinction.

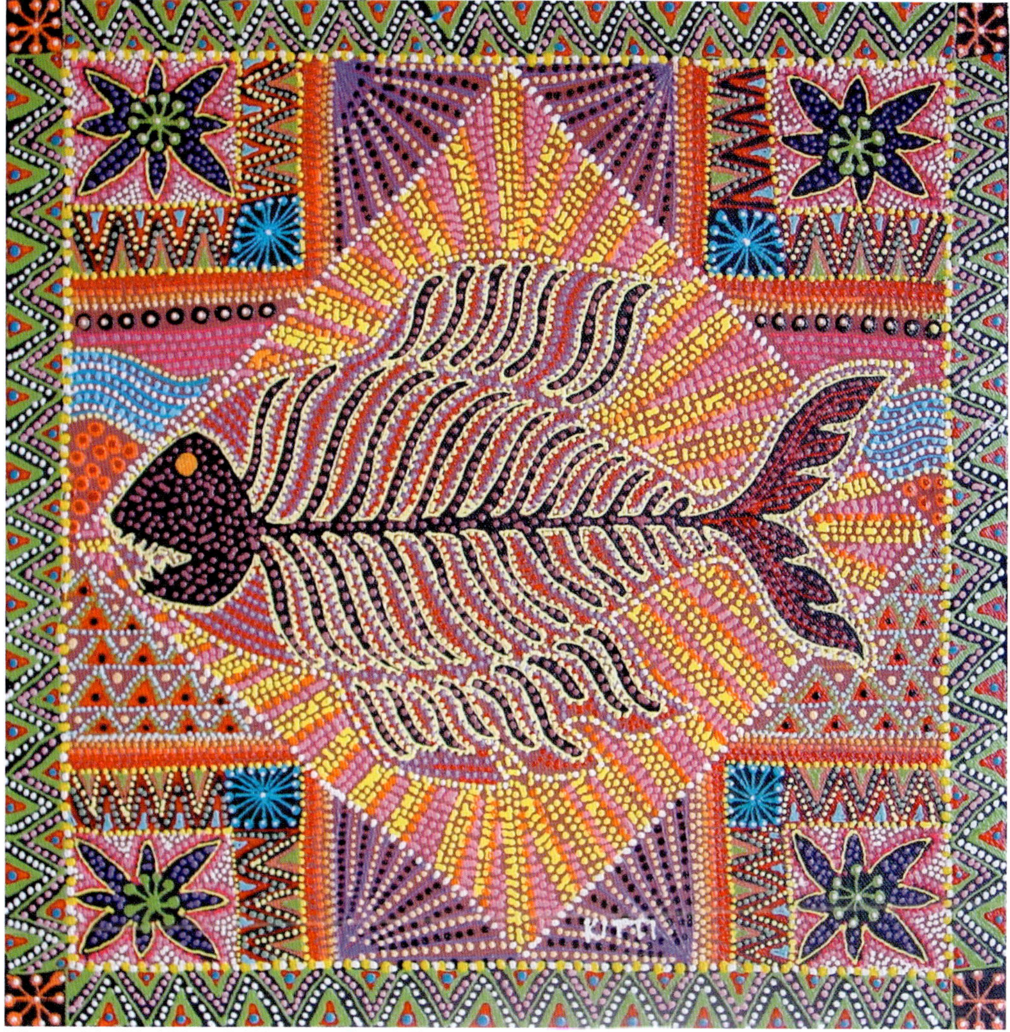

Figure 34: Kitti Narod: *Happened and Gone* (2005). 30 x 30 cm. Acrylic on canvas. (Private Collection).

Happened and Gone pictures a fossilised fish. Here is a life that was extinguished millions of years ago. Relatively static, patchwork elements frame the central skeletal creature. Its bones are revealed within its body outline, rather as Aboriginal "x-ray" paintings show backbones and skeletons inside the body of the person or animal portrayed. Kitti's fish skeleton, however, is radiant, silhouetted against a warm pink and brilliant yellow dotted diamond. How so? Two possible explanations come to mind. One is that a life once lived is wonderful and vibrant, even though it is lived no longer: the creature may be "gone" now, but at least it "happened" and doubtless enjoyed itself in the process, and this is a positive thing, worth celebrating in art. Another explanation might be that the creature that once

37

existed and was believed to have "gone", that is, to be extinct, in fact did not die out at all but lives on. Such is the case of the "living fossil" fish, the coelacanth. These creatures were thought to have first come into existence an inconceivable four hundred million years ago, flourished around two hundred and forty million years ago and faded into extinction about seventy million years ago. Fossils indicate that coelacanths ranged from about six inches to five feet in length and inhabited lakes, swamps, seas and oceans in the prehistoric world.

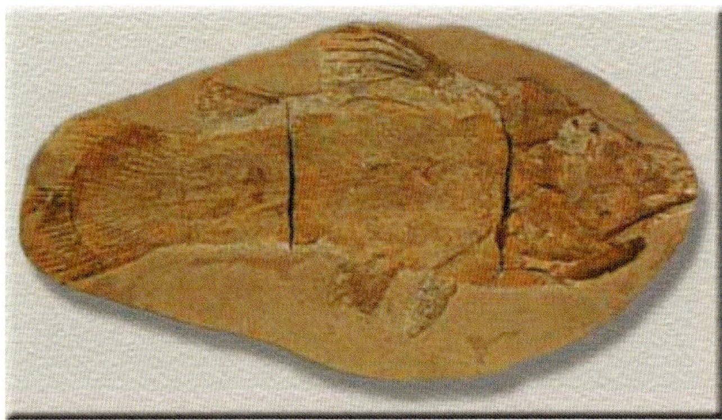

Figure 35: Coelacanth fossil, www.dinofish.com

Fishy, flat and very dead, our fossilised specimen above is no radiant remembrance of a life once lived. But look below.

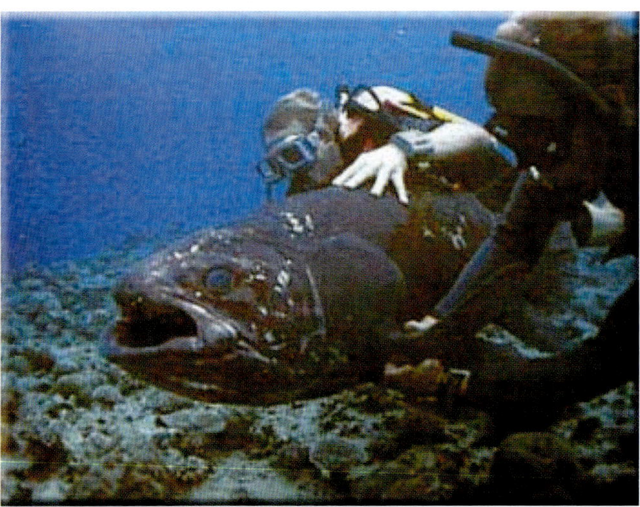

Figure 36: live coelacanth with divers, www.dinofish.com

So when is extinct not extinct? Answer: when you find a live one. Coelacanth has good reason to be radiant. After its ancestors had been skulking for millennia at the bottom of the oceans, a live coelacanth shattered the myth of its extinction by being fished out of the sea just off

South Africa in 1938. Since then, more specimens and colonies have been documented, mainly in the waters east of Africa, around Madagascar, and once, in 1998, near Manado Tua Island, Sulawesi, Indonesia. Coelacanth is exciting not only because it means that pre-history is alive and well in our day and age but also because the creature was once thought to be the ancestor of four-legged, land-dwelling animals, a category that includes human beings. Amongst other unique characteristics, the coelacanth possesses unusual paired fins that move similarly to our own arms and legs.

So Coelacanth, admittedly not a pretty fish, could be our ancient ancestor, living still alongside us even now. As such, he would be truly worthy of an Australian Aboriginal Dreaming. He gives the lie to the idea that extinction is forever. Kitti Narod's fossil fish is perhaps radiant in the knowledge that he has "happened" but in fact not "gone" as people imagine, but rather continues to enjoy his life in privileged seclusion.

With his Aboriginally inspired dot paintings, Kitti Narod has found a style of his own that is unique in the context of modern Thai painting. His work sees nature and transforms it for us magically. Kitti's nature is instantly recognisable, but not because it is a realistic representation of what we see. This is a dream-reality, perhaps, a particular kind of surrealism or super-realism that removes the real to beyond the every-day and infuses it with a lasting aesthetic brilliance and mystical quality. "Magic Realism", the American Surrealists' name for their art, would perhaps not be a bad description of Kitti's artistic vision.

Kitti Narod's world is not deformed, angry or imposing. It is joyful, radiating a serenity born of the artist's understanding and enjoyment of the natural world. And his product is visually attractive, too. Viewers stand back to take in the whole impression, or they may practically press their noses to the canvas when looking at the details. They appreciate the subject-matter at a surface level or else enquire into deeper content and affinities. However they approach Kitti Narod's art, viewers generally step away from it feeling better about the world and themselves than before they made the contact. This is a great achievement for a young painter.

Kitti Narod is not content to let his art stand still, however. Take a look at his **Blue Forest** of 2004.

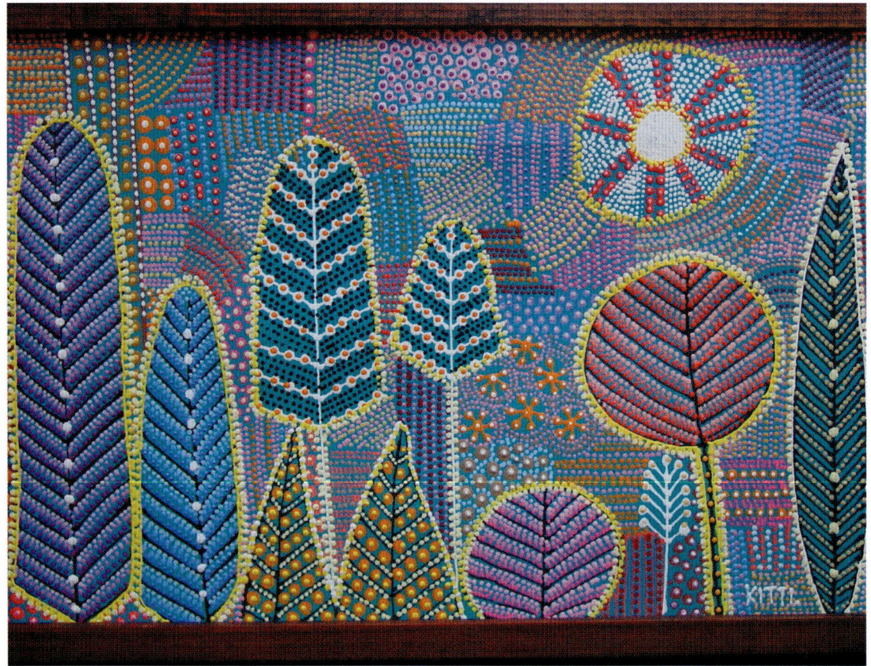

Figure 37: Kitti Narod: **Blue Forest** (2004). 25.3 x 40 cm. Acrylic on Canvas. Framed. (Private Collection).

40

Stylised trees in blues and blue-greens are silhouetted against a patchwork blue sky lit by a blue sun. Kitti's trees are abstractions, elementary tree forms, essence of tree, if you like. This is taken a step further by *Sunlight and Winter*.

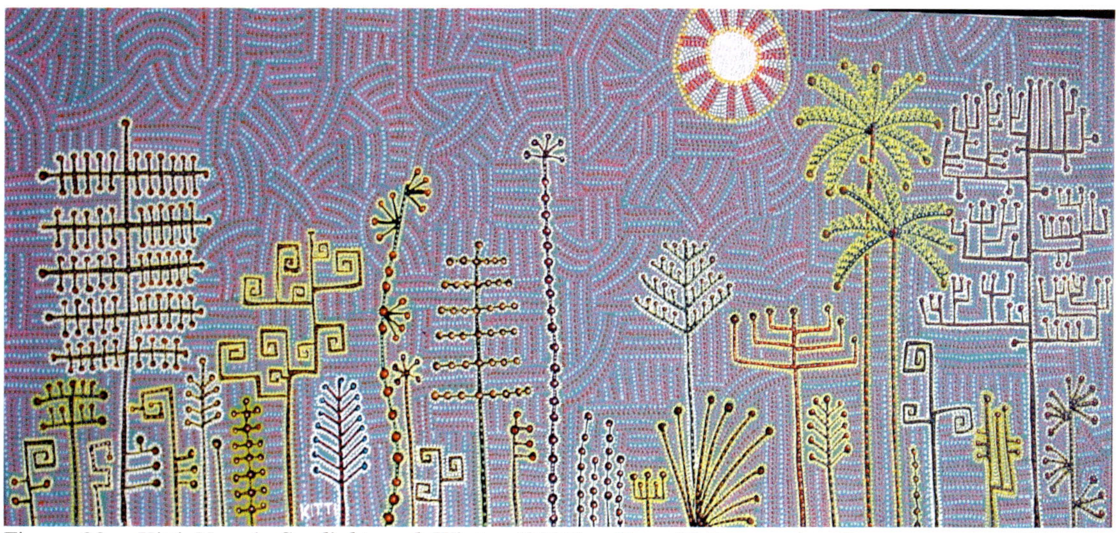

Figure 38: Kitti Narod: *Sunlight and Winter* (2005). 71 x 30.5 cm. Acrylic on canvas. (Private collection).

Kitti Narod has always lived in Thailand, where there is no winter as Europeans or North Americans know it. Although stylised, his *Blue Forest* vegetation is still typically tropical, with thick, fleshy abundant leaves. *Sunlight and Winter*, by contrast, juxtaposes tropical palm trees with the leafless, highly abstract tree shapes that for Kitti evoke the winter landscape in northern countries. These slender, angular tree shapes reduce the essence of tree to minimalist proportions. They are set against a background that is, for Kitti, neutral in both colour and design. The painting represents a new departure for the artist, opening pathways towards an evolution in his subjects and style.

The Surrealist Movement that began in Paris in the 1920s emphasised dreaming and the unconscious as sources of inner truth for the creative activity of the writers and artists who became associated with the movement. Salvador Dalí, for example, claims to have painted a more or less photographic transcription of dreams. Joan Miró was formally associated with Surrealism for a short time only, but he is generally regarded as one of the movement's leading figures. Miró's unique style, often called "biomorphic abstraction", features shapes and bursts of sharp colour that seem to float across a neutral background. Miró suggests, he does not explain. The viewer is free to link the painter's abstractions with whatever

41

associations these evoke in his, the viewer's, own mind, both at a conscious level and subconsciously. Miró attracts on three levels at the very least: visually, because his work is aesthetically pleasing; intellectually, because it is intriguing; and intuitively, because it evokes sensations, memory and imagination in the viewer. Many observers of Kitti Narod's ***Untitled Dream*** claim that the painting reminds them of Miró's work.

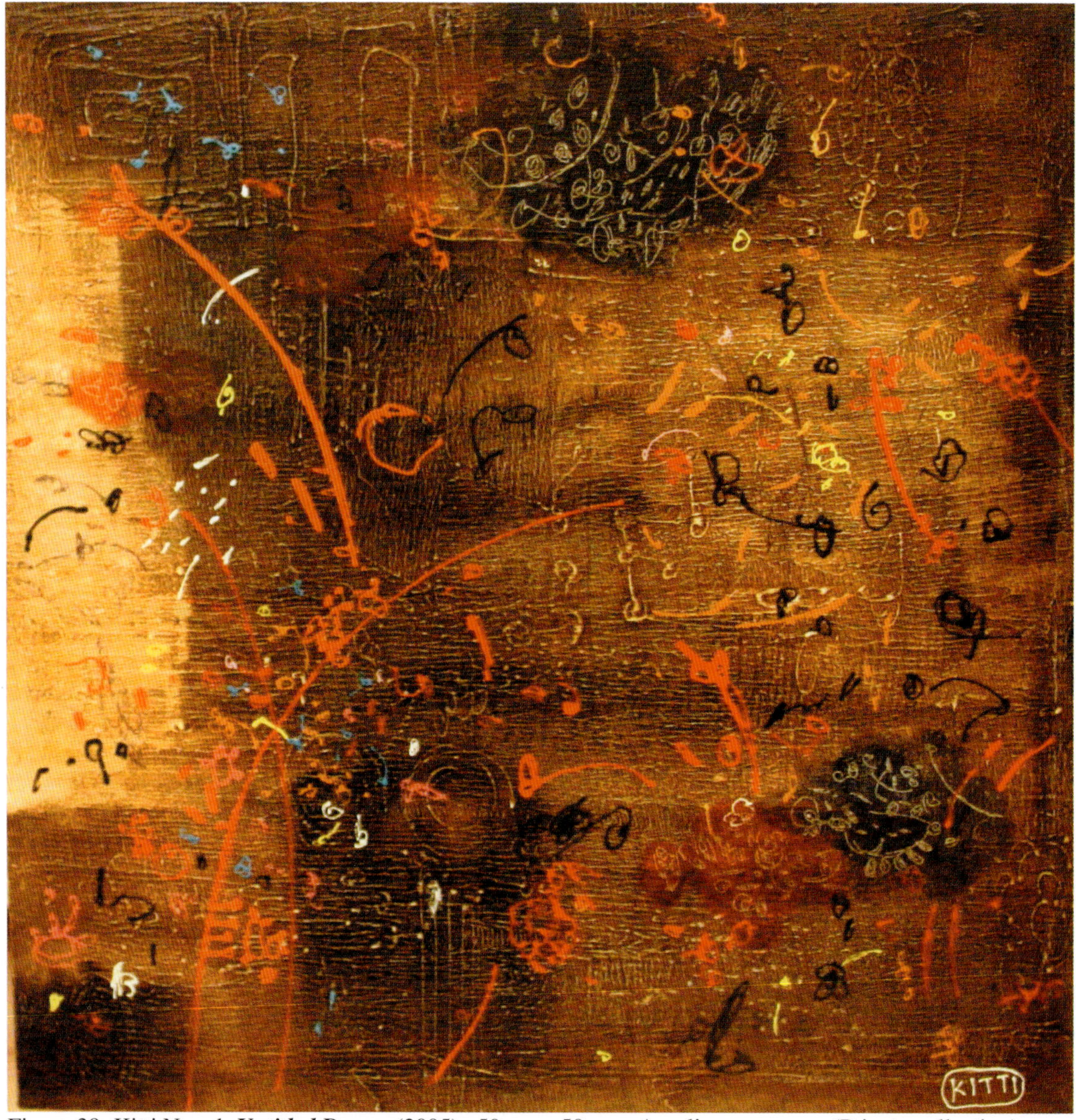

Figure 39: Kitti Narod: ***Untitled Dream*** (2005). 50 cm x 50 cm. Acrylic on canvas. (Private collection).

Since ancient days, dreams have been interpreted, often as omens for the future. Since Sigmund Freud, dreams have been interpreted in a more clinical context as messages of past trauma giving rise to present mental imbalances. Dreams can be interpreted, but they cannot be rationally explained. There are no hard and fast, one-on-one equivalences between the dream and reality. Similarly, Kitti Narod's ***Untitled Dream*** is suggestive, not explanatory. The painting draws on fantasy, memory and the irrational. Lines, squiggles and playful, amorphous designs are painted in a bright, very limited colour range or scratched out against a flat, neutral background. There are the merest suggestions of organic shapes, flowers or animals. Kitti Narod freely admits that, among modern western painters, Kandinsky and Miró are his favourites and have influenced his painting.

Kitti is fortunate in that he is an artist who enjoys his work. Painting gives him pleasure. His dot paintings involve much preparation: sketching, planning and thinking designs through. The actual painting work is laborious and exhausting. When he finishes a dot painting, Kitti's satisfaction comes from seeing a work of art come to life and from the very act of creation itself: starting from the very small, a mere dot, a whole world evolves within the confines of the canvas. This world then speaks to others, to Kitti's public. The satisfaction he derives from a painting like ***Unititled Dream*** is different. Here, he paints more freely than when using the dot technique. The work grows in harmony with the painter's mood. Kitti explains that his abstracts are less planned, because he creates in the moment, working from within. Surrealists would claim that Kitti is working from his subconscious mind, expressing the meaning of his work as it were automatically, without conscious manipulation of raw inspiration. Kitti is no theorist. ***Untitled Dream*** is not programmed. But Surrealist theorists would be pleased with him.

Compared to ***Untitled Dream***, ***Bangkok Crazy City*** relies marginally less on suggestion; its inferences are more specific, less ambiguous.

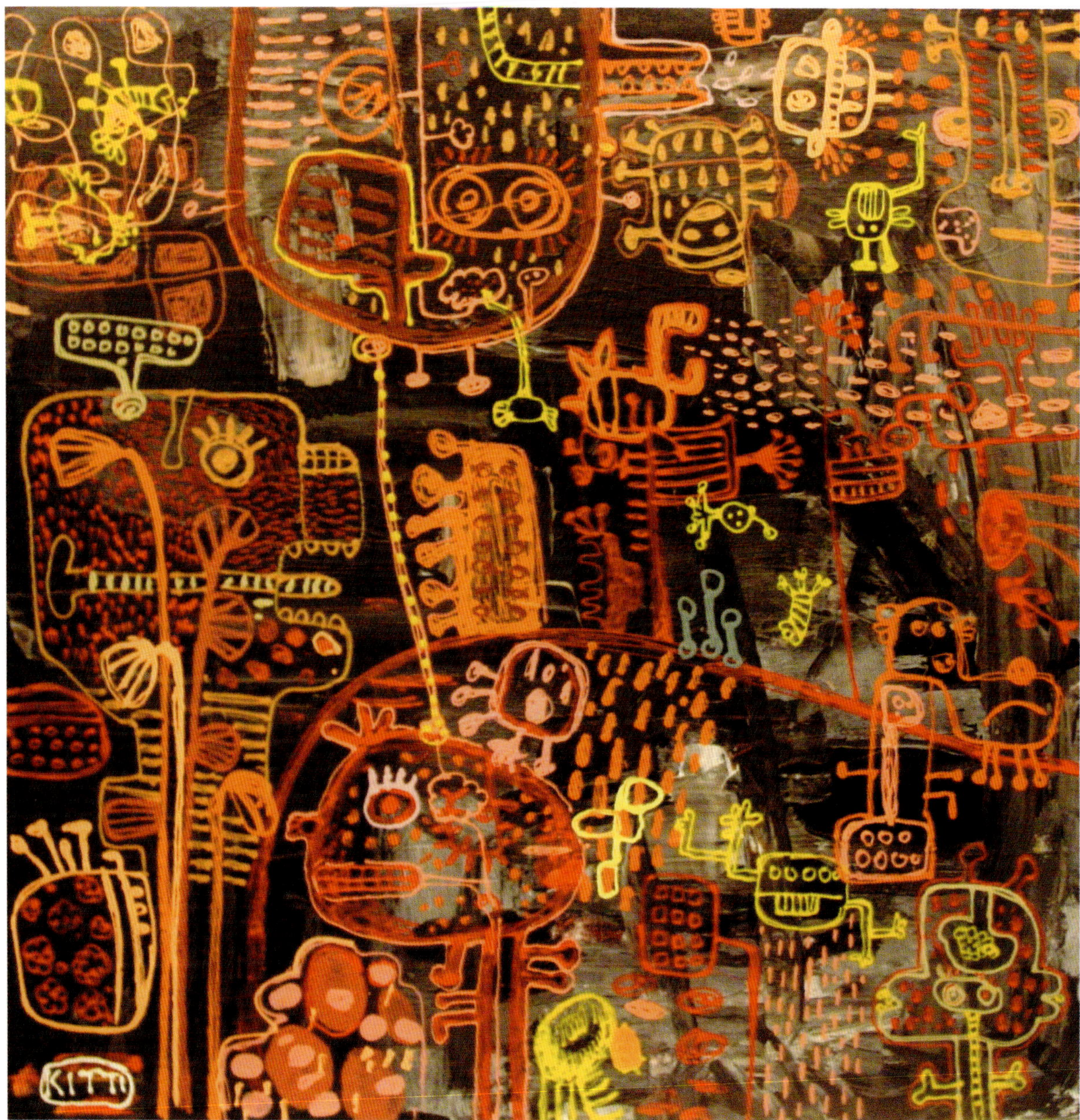

Figure 40: Kitti Narod: ***Bangkok Crazy City*** (2005). 50 x 50 cm. Acrylic on canvas. (Private collection).

The crowded canvas of ***Bangkok Crazy City*** mirrors the Thai capital's frenzied jumble of shacks and skyscrapers, dilapidated shop-houses and glitzy modern shopping complexes, crisscrossed by alleyways and motorways, sky-trains and subway trains, thronged with every type of motorized vehicle imaginable and folk on foot buying and selling everything from dumplings to DVDs. Add to these ingredients breathtaking Buddhist shrines and temples both great and small, together with Bangkok's tropical sunshine, smog and torrential downpours, the majestic Chao Phraya River crowded with vessels of every size and shape and the ethnic mix of local Thais and Chinese rubbing shoulders with visitors from everywhere, and you will understand why Kitti Narod would call Bangkok a crazy city.

As Miró adapted fantastical shapes as if from children's art, Narod too combines these here with cartoon-like figures, sometimes nightmarish, always a step beyond rationality, painted against his darkly neutral background in intranquil orange, red and yellow tones. There are "x-ray" views of human faces where we seem to be able to see the thoughts inside their heads, though "reading" these thoughts is another matter. There are distorted machine creatures and insect-like figures crowded together with cyber-dots, rain-showers and fearsome, toothy creations, perhaps part bird or part crocodile, one of which, to the left of the canvas, seems to have swallowed up the vegetation that Bangkok's rapid growth has asphalted over.

Kitti Narod's Bangkok is crazy indeed, but vital, dynamic, pulsating, ever-changing. If faced with the choice between evolution or extinction, Bangkok, living entity that this city is for this artist, will opt for evolution. As does Kitti himself, adapting his technique in step with his own changing vision. The magical quality of his work is retained, however. Kitti Narod's idiom has, for the moment, changed, but the artist continues to express his "dreaming", his own personal vision of his world, his life and the world he shares with us, his viewers, through his art.

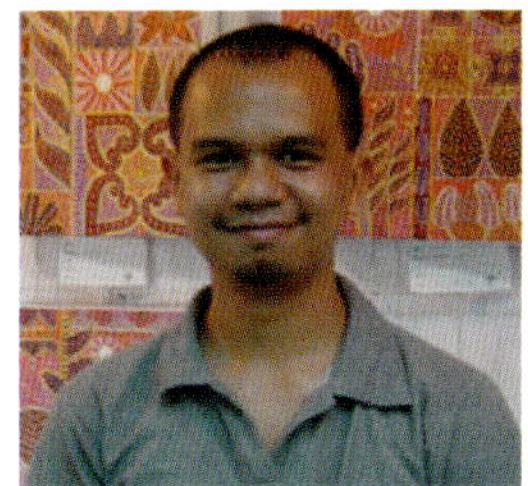

Photograph courtesy of Thai Fine Art Ltd.

About the Artist

Kitti Narod was born on January 18th 1976 in Chai Nat, a small, farming village not far from the city of Nakhon Sawan, which is strategically located about 300 km north of Bangkok in the Central Plains area at the confluence of an assortment of waterways that run down from the mountains of the north and west to merge into the mighty Chao Phraya River.

Kitti started drawing at a young age and soon found that this was what he did best. There are no other artists as such in his family, but his mother, Somkiat, helped guide the young painter's hand, and two of his elementary school teachers, Ms Panthip Muangneung and another he remembers only as Prompaeng, encouraged his first artistic efforts. Kitti's parents were not enthusiastic about his decision to study art at college. Even though they did not insist he carry on farming rice in the family tradition, they had a more institutional career in mind for their son, perhaps as a teacher, civil servant, or in the military or the police force. At the same time, they did not oppose Kitti's career decision, and it was with the blessing of his mother, Somkiat, his father, Sawat, and his younger brother, Anut, that Kitti, after completing his studies at the Archiwa Nakhom Sawan College in 1996, left home to set out for art college and the Rajamonkong Institute of Technology in Bangkok.

1998 saw Kitti's first exhibition at the Bangkok Wittalayai Phochan Art College Anniversary Exhibition, followed in 2000 by the All Thai Alternative Exhibit in Bangkok. 2004 was a breakthrough year for Kitti's work, in that he exhibited not only in the prestigious River City Shopping Complex (well respected at home and abroad for its permanent exhibition and sales of antique furniture, statuary and paintings as well as for its periodic promotions of young Thai artists), and at the Bangkok Art Market, but also because this was the year his talent was "discovered" by Thai Fine Art Ltd and shown outside of Thailand for the first time at the Bath Christmas Fair in England. Kitti's international exposure was enhanced in

2004 and 2005 via Thai Fine Art Ltd's Internet Gallery and Shop, and by a series of exhibitions in the UK: the organiser of the May 2005 Raw Arts Festival in Islington, London, singled out Kitti's paintings from among Thai Fine Art Ltd's artists for exclusive exhibition at the Festival; Thai Fine Art Ltd's debut solo show at the Zizi Gallery in London's Mayfair then strongly featured Kitti's work (June-July 2005), followed by a repeat performance at the Dundas Street Gallery in Edinburgh (July 2005). Visitors to all these events were fascinated by the novelty and intricate workmanship of Kitti's paintings, many of which now belong to private collections all over Britain. Thai Fine Art Ltd's presence at the Manchester Art Show in October 2005 will also showcase Kitti's work. Kitti Narod is represented in the UK and on the Internet exclusively by Thai Fine Art Ltd via www.thai-fine-art.com and at periodic exhibitions and shows in Britain and on the continent.

A modest, soft-spoken young man, nearing thirty and unattached, Kitti Narod enjoys the company of his friends. When painting, however, he prefers to be alone, working in his studio above the Magic Art Gallery he shares with other artists, listening perhaps to jazz, Thai folk music or, more recently, to western classics. Painting in the dot technique is exhausting. The initial inspiration calls for a series of detailed preparatory sketches where not even the smallest dot placement is left to chance. Doing the actual painting is strenuous and time-consuming but at the same time cathartic. Kitti explains that his concentration is so intense that it sweeps all other extraneous matters out of his mind, so that, when a work-session is finished, he feels a sense of relief and is able to think more clearly than before. Perhaps as meditation according to Buddhist teaching clears the mind and heart and helps the practitioner face the world in a better spiritual way.

When inspiration strikes, Kitti works quickly until the work is done. Each step proceeds methodically and there is no need for turning back or for correction. Kitti works confidently and without consulting others. Critics may carp or praise once the work is done, but no changes will be made. The artist is secure in the knowledge of what his work is worth.

The acrylic paintings by Kitti Narod are inspired by Aboriginal dot paintings. The dot technique evokes the feeling of movement inspired by the natural settings of their subjects. The natural shapes are reduced and transformed into free-form images reminiscent of Indian and Aboriginal art. Inspired by his art, Kitti Narod adds his imagination and skill to create these works.   After taking a look at many different styles of painting, Kitti came upon the dots on dots Australian Aboriginal art and found that this spoke to him personally as an artist. Themes from nature, flowers, fruits, leaves, waves, trees, the sea and sea creatures are interwoven in colour schemes drawn from the blue of the sky and the warm palette inspired by Kitti's tropical sun.
(**Thai Fine Art Ltd on Kitti Narod**)

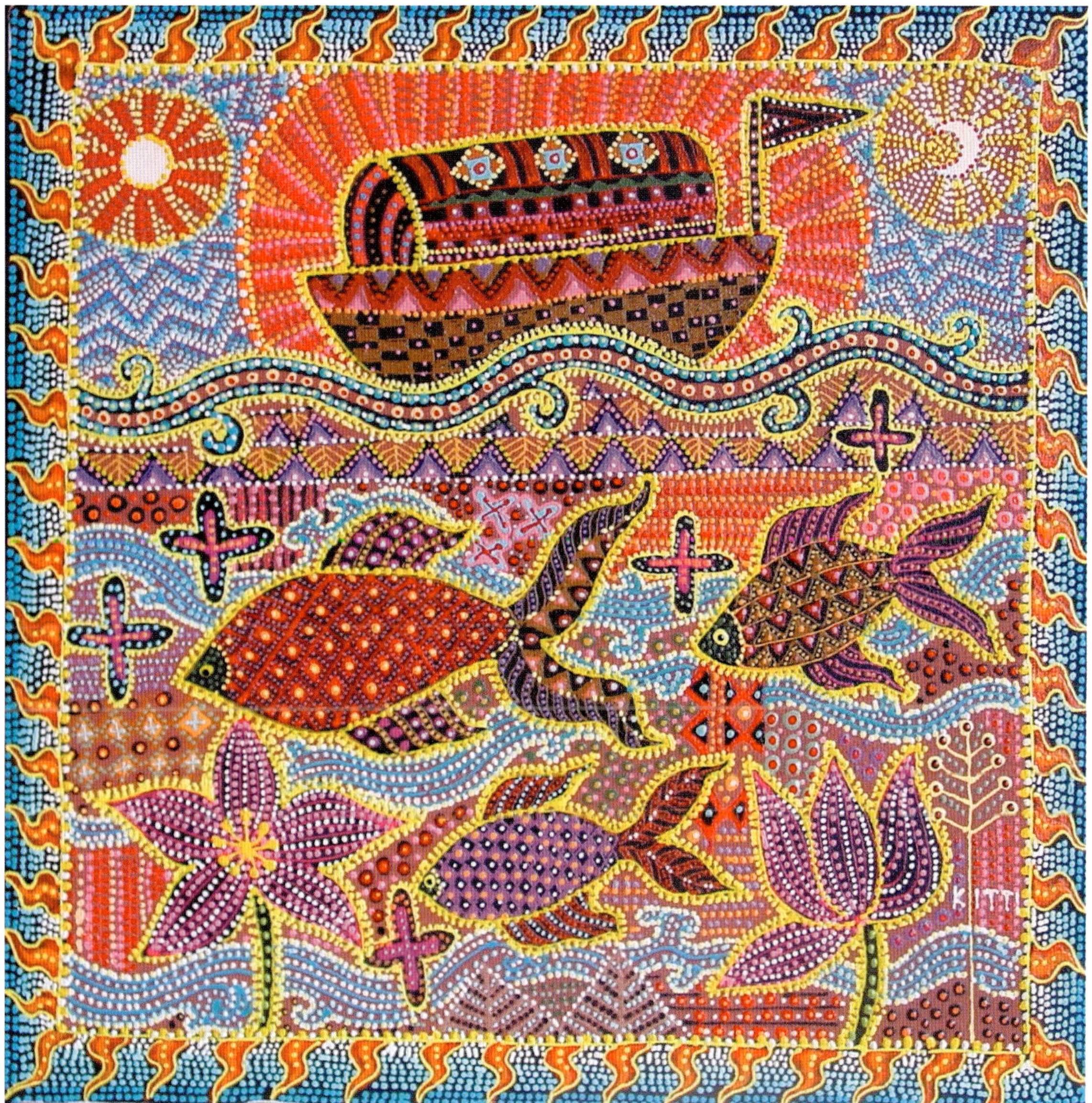

Figure 41: Kitti Narod: *Destine* (2005). 30 x 30 cm. Acrylic on canvas.

Looking at one of Kitti Narod's dot paintings is pleasurable enough as a visual experience; inquiring minds, however, will always wonder *why* Kitti's elements are grouped the way they are and what they "mean" to the artist on a symbolic, spiritual or intellectual level. Kitti guards his technical secrets closely, but he is happy to explain his symbolism. A personal interview with the artist yielded information about *Destine* that is useful in understanding what goes into his other dot paintings as well.

Destine's boat has absolutely nothing to do with Noah's Ark, which is what a viewer raised in the Judeo-Christian way of looking at things might have been thinking. "Life is like a boat," Kitti declares; life's journey may be stormy or calm, depending on whatever destiny decrees. With Buddhist equanimity, Kitti accepts life's ups and downs; the boat that is his life and our lives is radiant; life is a gift and wondrous, celebrated here in art.

Both sun and moon light up the sky: this lends eternity to the picture, the boat sails on and on, through times of joy and sorrow, as one life leads through to another in the Buddhist creed of reincarnation until Nirvana is attained. The sun for Kitti is especially significant: it is the cosmic creator, the life-force without which nothing on earth would exist. This hot, bright, tropical sun is a salient feature of Kitti's dot paintings.   Even the diluted, blue-toned sun of *Sunlight and Winter* dominates that painting's chilly sky.

In the water, cross-shapes represent coral-flowers. Fish are strong and beautiful. Kitti fondly recalls times with his father when, as a boy, he visited rivers and the sea-shore, looking at fish and shells and all manner of water plants and creatures, learning, even at that young age, how meaningful these are. Kitti's affection for fish is clear from how often and how well they are portrayed in his art. We need only think back to *Pacific Party*.

Life's voyage is framed in *Destine* by a painted border of flames, a motif that is both prevalent and significant in Buddhist art.

About the Author

Born in Scotland at the height of WWII and educated in England and the USA, Dr Felicity Rodner spent over thirty years in Venezuela with her husband, three daughters and an assortment of pet dogs, cats, tortoises, birds and fish. While in Venezuela, she became fluent in Spanish, wrote and successfully submitted her Harvard doctoral thesis, took a law degree by correspondence from London University, was active in local and expat groups and taught English and German at high school and university level as well as privately.

Upon definitively returning to Britain in 2002, Dr Rodner found new pathways unexpectedly leading her eastwards. One chance family visit to Thailand sparked an enthusiasm in Dr Rodner and her youngest daughter, Vicky, that prompted further visits and an in-depth acquaintance with Thai art and culture. Vicky married Suebpong Khunapramot, whom she had met while teaching English in Thailand. She also founded her own company, Thai Fine Art Ltd, in 2004 to promote young Thai artists by exhibiting and selling their work internationally, with special emphasis on the talents of Kitti Narod. Part of Dr Rodner's contribution to this latter effort takes the form of this booklet, which is the first published study of the importance of Australian Aboriginal dot techniques in Narod's paintings. The book starts with an introduction to Thai art that should prove useful to western readers who may not be familiar with this subject. Dr Rodner then highlights those aspects of Australian Aboriginal art that seem relevant to Kitti's dot technique and proceeds to take a detailed look at his most interesting pieces, leading on to the latest developments in the artist's style and subject-matter. The author's familiarity with the artist and his work provides intriguing insights that should interest any art enthusiast who appreciates cross-cultural influences and has an eye for aesthetic originality.

Thai Dreamings: Australian Aboriginal Inspirations in the Paintings of Kitti Narod was published by Felicity A. Rodner under the auspices of Thai Fine Art Ltd and printed by Permanent Printing Ltd in Hong Kong. 2005. Copyright © 2005 Felicity A. Rodner.

Unless otherwise credited, all photographs by the author.

Some Pages from the Sketchbooks
of Kitti Narod

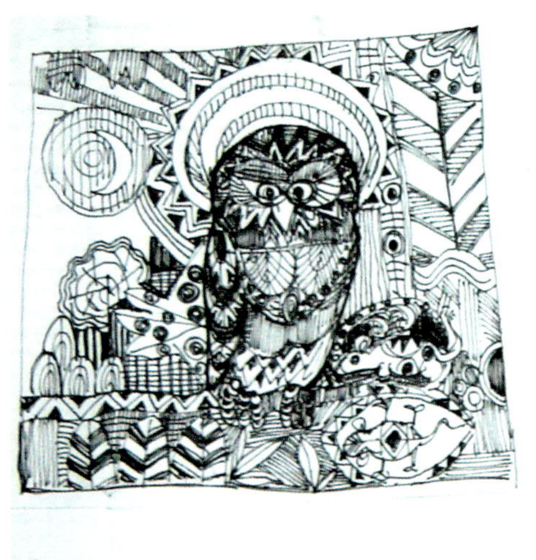

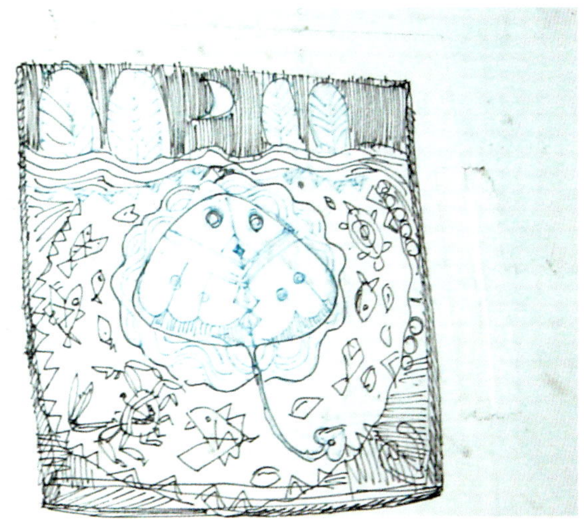

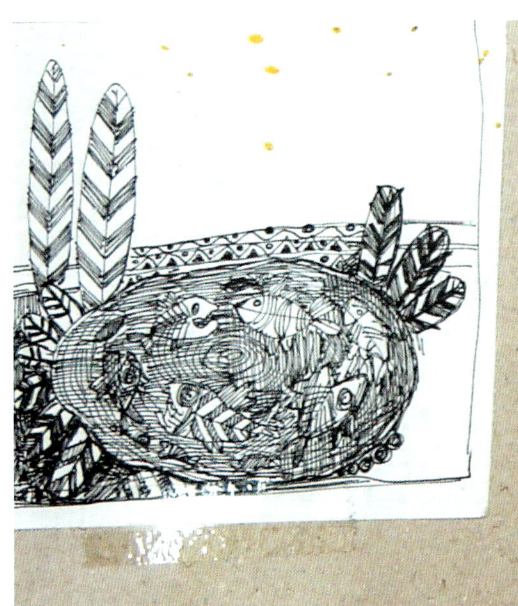

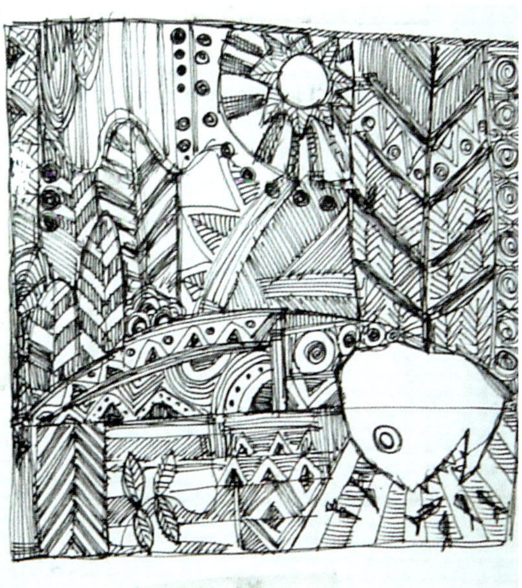

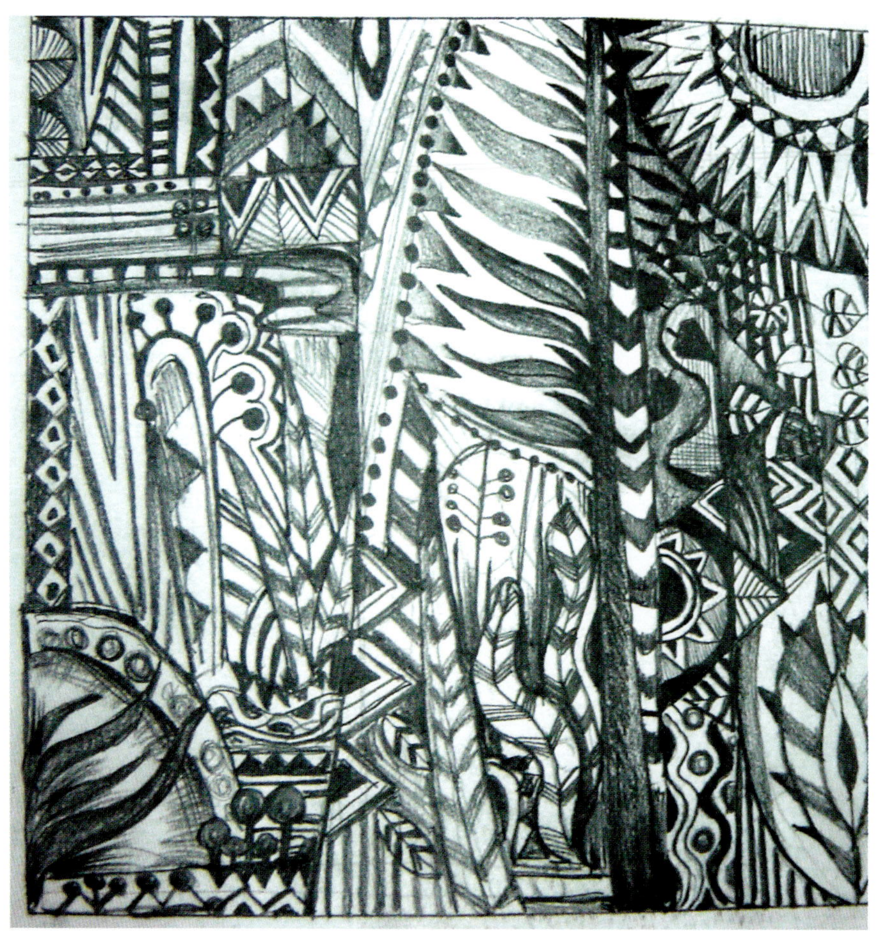

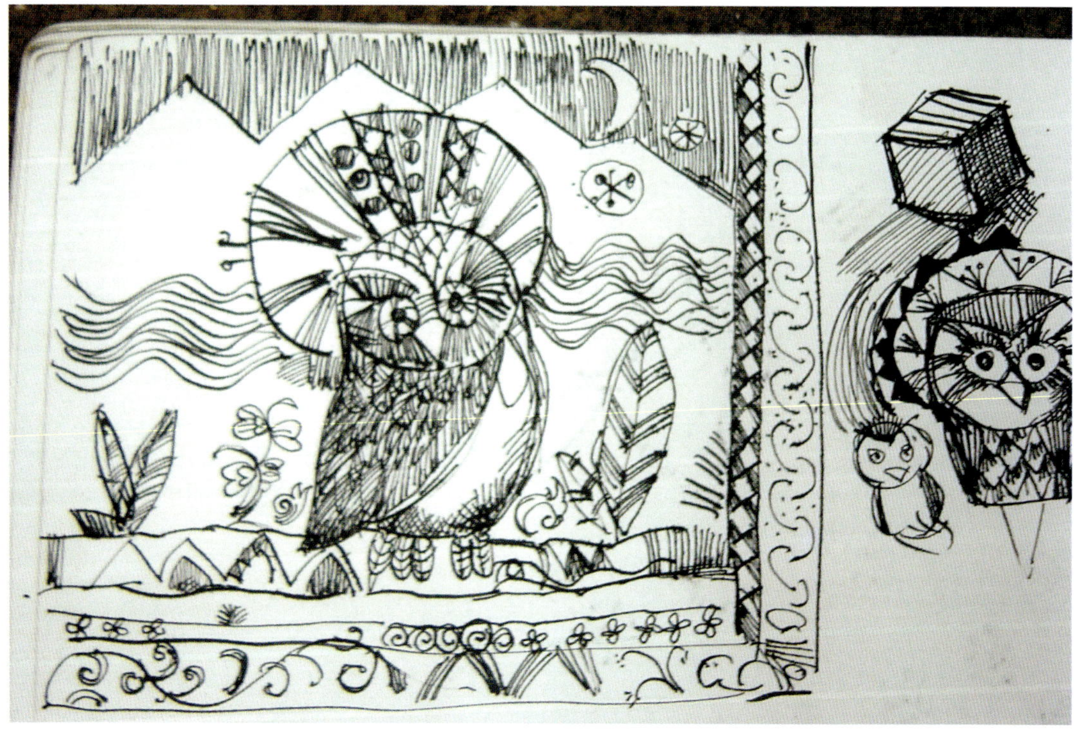

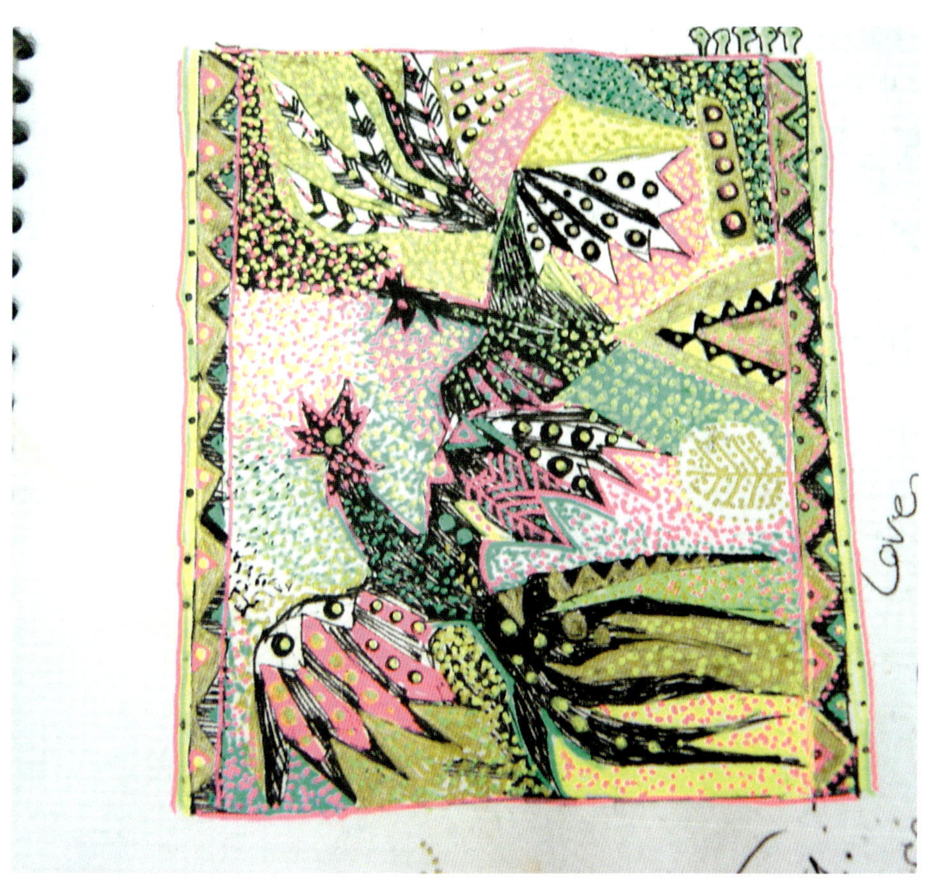

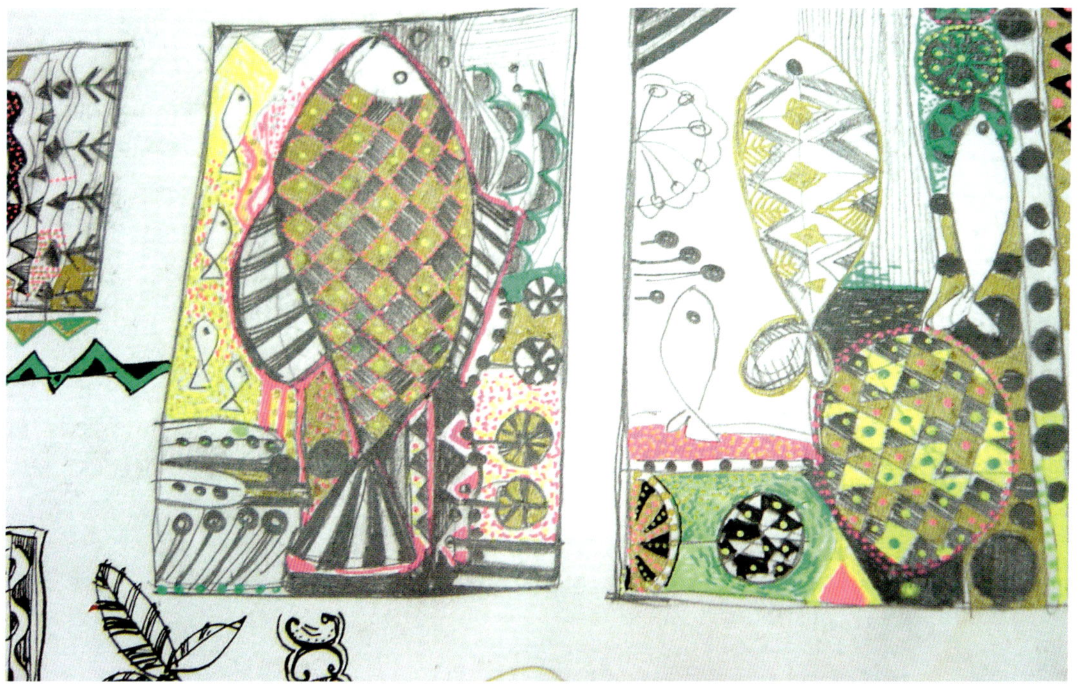

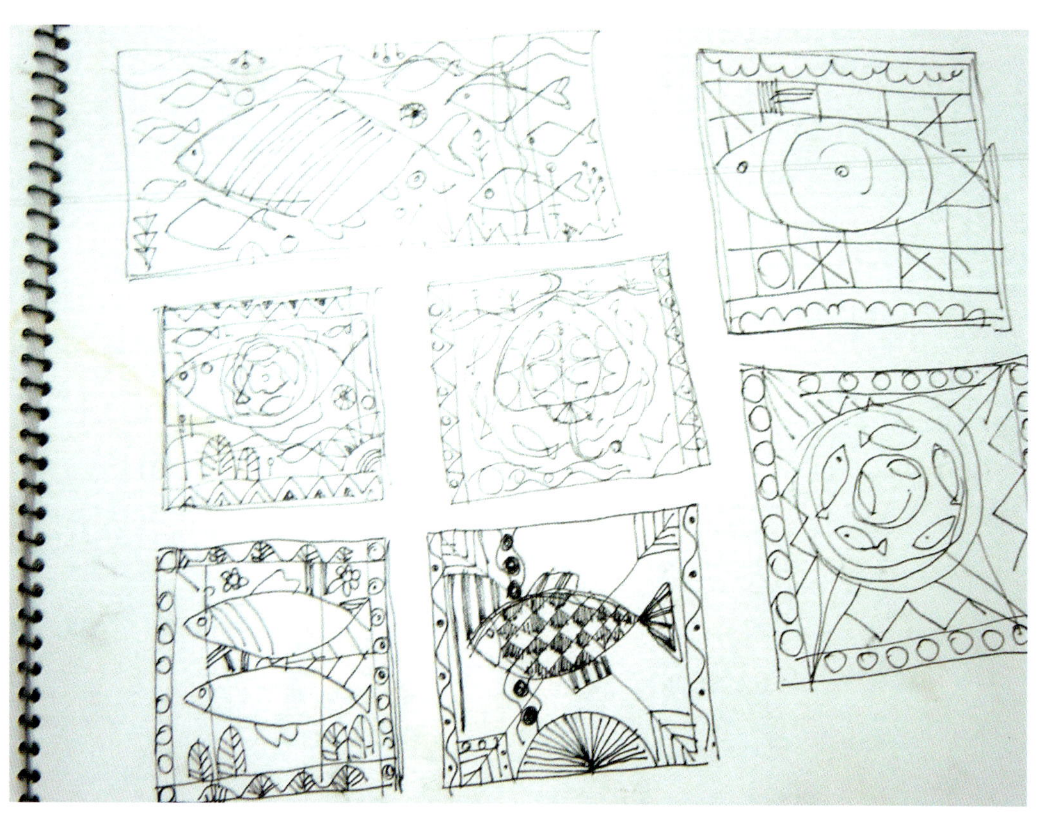

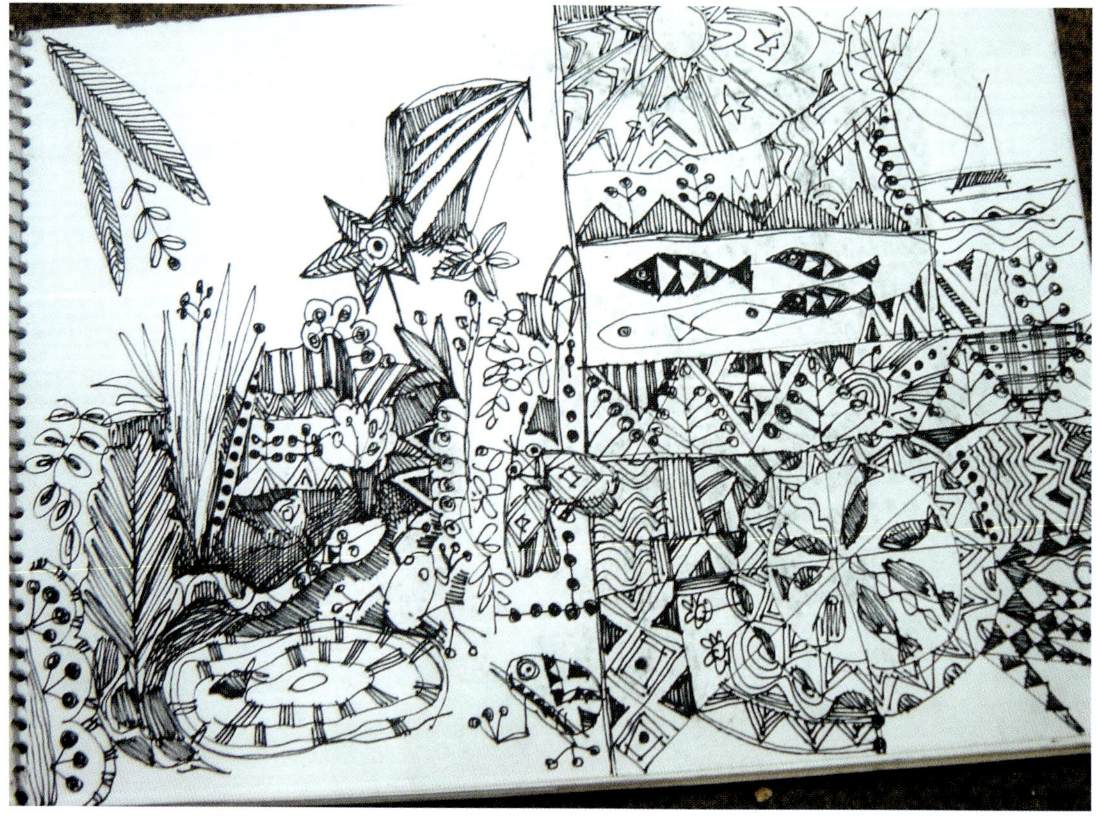

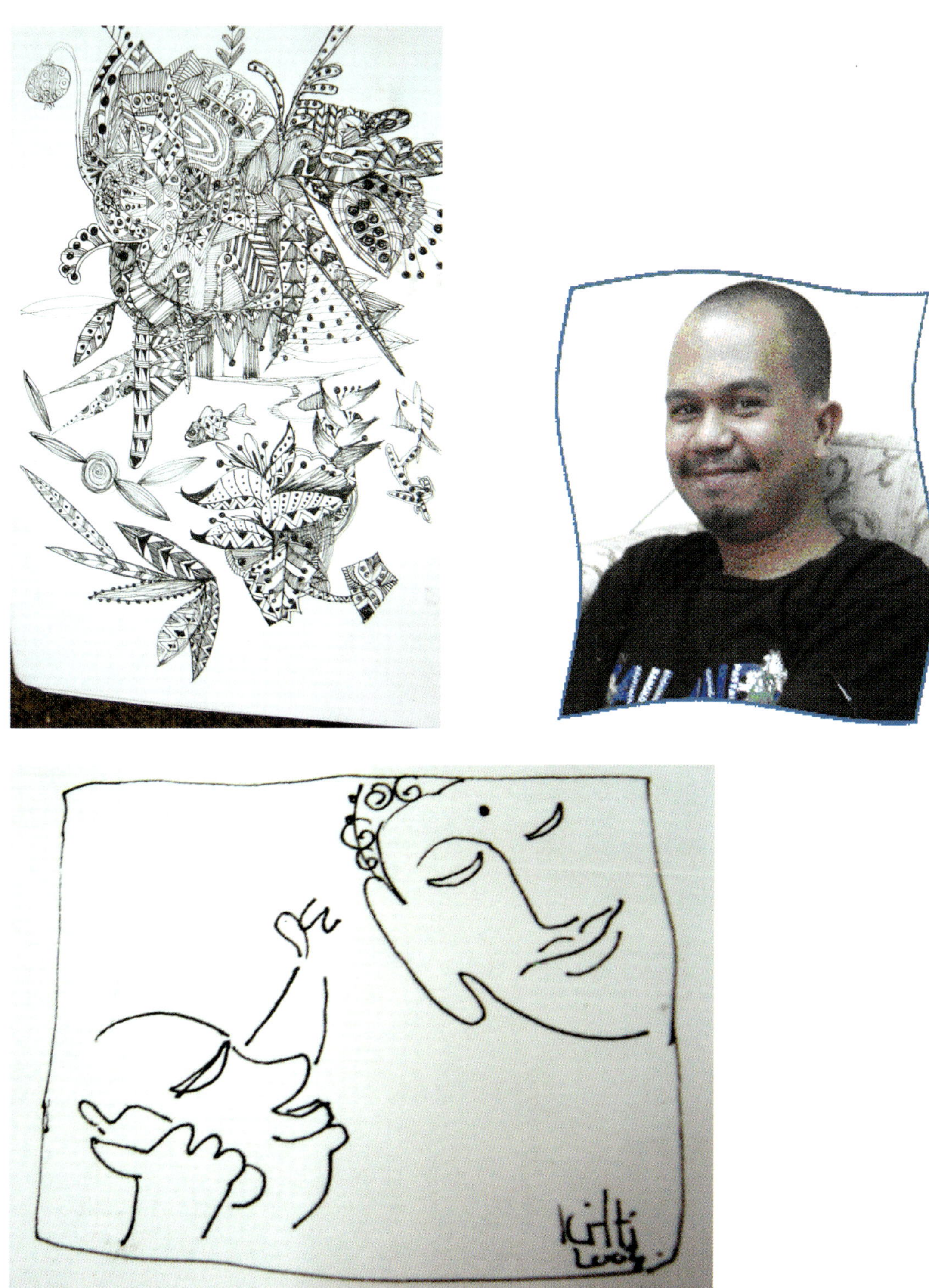

Kitti Narod's sketchbook pages courtesy of Thai Fine Art Ltd.

Select Bibliography

19th Art Exhibition, Faculty of Painting, Sculpture and Graphic Arts, Silpakorn University, Bangkok, Thailand, 2002 (exhibition catalogue).

Apinan Poshyananda: *Modern Art in Thailand*. Oxford University Press, Singapore, 1992.

Bangkok Post: "Masterstroke by Master Painter. Chalermchai Kositpipat digs deep to create a masterpiece", Bangkok, Thailand, 28-7-2005.

Caruana, Wally: *Aboriginal Art*. Thames and Hudson, World of Art Series, London and New York, 1993, 2003.

Chalermchai Kositpipat: *Painting Pictures, Painting Life* (in Thai). Amarin Printing and Publishing Plc, Bangkok, Thailand, 2000.

Kreangkri Vongpitirat and Thongchai Srisukprasert: *Rhupadhram Thai Namadhram Thai.* The Silom Galleria, Bangkok, Thailand, 2001 (exhibition catalogue).

Loschmann, Jorg: "Identities versus Globalisation?" Fine Art Magazine, Chiang Mai, Thailand, March 2004, Volume 1, No. 3.

Microsoft Encarta Encyclopedia, 2003. *Joan Miró, Salvador Dalí, Surrealism; coelacanth.*

Morphy, Howard: *Aboriginal Art.* Phaidon Press, London and New York, Art and Ideas Series, 1998, 1999, 2001, 2003.

Pettifor, Steven: *Flavours. Thai Contemporary Art.* Thavibu Gallery Co. Ltd, Bangkok, Thailand. 2003.

Phatyos Buddhacharoen: *From Limestone.* Faculty of Painting, Sculpture and Graphic Art, Silpakorn University, Bangkok, Thailand, 1998 (exhibition catalogue).

Pinaree Sanpitak: ***Breast and Beyond*** (in English and Thai). Publisher unknown. Exhibition catalogue for Bangkok University Art Gallery, Chulalongkorn University Art Center and Open Arts Space, Bangkok, Thailand, 2002.

Sakarin Krue-on: ***Yellow Simple***. The Silom Galleria, Bangkok, Thailand, 2001 (exhibition catalogue).

Taylor, Pamela York: ***Beasts, Birds and Blossoms in Thai Art (The Asia Collection)***. OUP S.E. Asia. 1995.

Van Beek, Steve and Tettoni, Luca Invernizzi: ***The Arts of Thailand***. Periplus Editions, Hong Kong, 1999, 2000; text and photography from 1985, 1991.

Vichoke Mukdamanee: ***Universe: Life: Science***. Amarin Printing and Publishing Plc, Bangkok, Thailand, 1996 (exhibition catalogue).

www.abc.net.au: 16-8-2005: "Aboriginal astronomers see mythology in stars".
www.aboriginalaustralia.com
www.asia-art.net: Nikorn U-aksorn, Pornchai Lerttamasiri, Soraya Runckel.
www.austmus.gov.au: coelacanth.
www.bangkokpost.co.th: 28-7-2005: Wat Rong Khun.
www.buddhanet.net: The Wheel of Life and Death.
www.chiangmai-chiangrai.com: "Commemoration of King Naresuan".
www.dinofish.com: coelacanth.
www.exploratorium.edu/frogs/folklore: Frog mythology.
www.geocities.com : The Wheel of Life and Death.
www.howtoenjoy.co.uk: 2-7-2005.
www.owlpages.com
www.rama9art.org: Chalermchai Kositpipat.
www.thai-fine-art.com